NEW THEORIES ON THE BIRTH OF THE UNIVERSE

CHRISTOPHER LAMPTON

FRANKLIN WATTS
NEW YORK LONDON TORONTO SYDNEY
] 1989 [

Photographs courtesy of:
Hansen Planetarium: p. 8; Bettmann Archive:
pp. 15, 69; Granger Collection: pp. 18, 22, 155;
AIP/Niels Bohr Library: p. 25; The Archives,
California Institute of Technology: p. 30;
AT&T Bell Laboratories: p. 36; NASA: p. 40;
Yerkes Observatory Photograph, University of
Chicago, Williams Bay, Wis.: p. 44; American
Museum of Natural History: p. 53; Fermilab:
p. 61; UPI/Bettmann Newsphotos: pp. 76,
143, 147; Camera 5: p. 95 (Ken Regan); Photo
Researchers: p. 105 (SPL); National Optical
Astronomy Observatories: p. 126; MIT: p. 131.

Library of Congress Cataloging-in-Publication Data
Lampton, Christopher.
New theories on the birth of the universe /
by Christopher Lampton.
p. cm.
Bibliography: p.
Includes index.
Summary: An introduction to the various physical
theories believed to underlie the origins of the universe.
ISBN 0-531-10782-5
1. Cosmology—Juvenile literature. [1. Cosmology.
2. Universe.] I. Title
QB983.L35 1989
523.1—dc20   89-32008 CIP AC

CONTENTS

NEW THEORIES ON
THE BIRTH
OF THE UNIVERSE

From ancient times to the frontiers of modern cosmology, physics, and astronomy, scientists have probed the vast sky for clues to understanding the universe.

INTRODUCTION

Over the last quarter of a century, something very remarkable has happened. Scientists engaged in fundamental physics—the study of the ultimate nature of our universe—have begun to suspect that they are about to run out of new things to study. Within the next few decades, it is possible, some think, that they will come to understand our universe completely, or very nearly so. This doesn't mean (as we will see later in this book) that they will know every last detail about our universe. It means, rather, that they will know the basic, underlying rules that make our universe the way it is, the details of the program (if you will) that makes the cosmic computer run.

How has this understanding come about? By careful study of the origin of our universe, the moment some 18 to 20 billion years ago when the cosmos (of which our tiny Planet Earth is a part) was born, many believe, in an immense explosion that we refer to only half-jokingly as the Big Bang. By studying the birth of the universe, physicists and astronomers have begun to discover just what it is that makes us the way we are, why matter and energy behave the way they do, and why the universe is the way it is. Paradoxically, this understanding has, in turn, helped them to better understand the birth of the universe. In effect, the Big Bang has become the biggest physics laboratory that ever existed—or that could ever exist.

In this book, we'll tell you what scientists now think they know about the birth of our universe; we'll also tell you what they think they know about the universe as it is today and the particles that make up matter plus the even smaller particles that make up these particles. And we'll show you how these two, seemingly very different, types of knowledge have gone hand in hand in helping scientists to answer one of the most profound questions that philosophers (and ordinary human beings) have asked throughout the ages: What *is* the universe and why is it here?

ONE

COSMOLOGY

The universe is a very, *very* big place. It is, in fact, the biggest place that could possibly exist, since it contains within itself all other places. The universe contains everything in, well, the universe.

It would seem that understanding something as large and all-encompassing as the universe might be beyond the reach of science, or at least beyond the reach of a single *field* of science. And yet this is not so. There is a field of science that studies the universe as a whole: its structure, its contents, its possible birth, its evolution, and its possible eventual death. That field of science is called *cosmology.*

In many ways, cosmology is a subfield of both astronomy and physics, and in this book we will sometimes use the names of the three fields interchangeably, depending on the context. But the aims of cosmology are much more ambitious than those of the sciences of which it is part. Cosmology aims to understand everything about the universe, no more or less. That doesn't mean that the cosmologist wants to know every little thing that takes place in the universe; those are mere details. The cosmologist, rather, wants to know the rules that explain *why* all of those things happen.

Cosmology is both a very old and a very young science. Long before the invention of written language, and *very* long before the advent of the formal set of procedures that we refer to today as science, human beings must have wondered about the vast and awe-inspiring cosmos that appeared in the night sky. We can only guess at the conjectures these ancient astronomers made about this cosmos. Perhaps they imagined that the stars and planets were fiery creatures that flitted about on errands that defied human imagining, or that the sky was a vast ceiling punctuated with small holes through which the light of some cosmic fire could be seen in flickering glimpses. Although their speculations are surely fascinating and poetic in their own right, it is doubtful that they bear much resemblance to modern theories, which are based on centuries of knowledge gained from the sciences of astronomy and physics.

The chief way in which these early "theories" of the universe differed from modern scientific theories is that they were based on the premise that the world beyond the reach of human beings—the world in the sky—was somehow different from the world on the ground, that it obeyed different rules. It was perfectly acceptable to postulate that the planets were strange flying creatures or that the sun was a magic chariot that flew daily across the heavens. Things were different in the sky. It was a world of magic, populated by gods.

The first attempts at a truly scientific theory of the universe were not made until about 2,500 years ago, by the ancient Greeks. Like the ancient astronomers before them, the Greeks were not hesitant to theorize about the nature of the universe. But at least some Greeks made a genuine attempt to ground their theories in observed fact, to explain what went on beyond the earthly realm not in terms of magic but in terms of the way objects behaved on the Planet Earth. A few Greek astronomers even made credible attempts to measure the size of the earth and the distances to the moon and the sun. The Greek mathematician Aristarchus proposed a description of the solar system remarkably like the one advanced 2,000 years later by the Polish astronomer Copernicus.

But the idea that the realm beyond the earth was somehow magical had not yet died completely. The great Greek philosopher Aristotle believed that heavenly objects were made of a special substance, called either *quintessence* ("fifth essence") or *ether*. This substance behaved quite differently from the four "elements"—earth, air, fire, and water—that he believed were the basis of our own world. For instance, heavenly objects naturally tended to move in a restless circular motion, revolving around the earth roughly once every twenty-four hours, while objects on earth tended not to move at all unless persuaded to do so by some force. And when they did move, they moved in a straight line—or so Aristotle believed.

Nonetheless, Aristotle was one of the earliest cosmologists. He developed a comprehensive view of our universe that survived in more or less its original form for the better part of 2,000 years. In terms of sheer staying power, Aristotle was certainly the most successful cosmologist of all time.

The Aristotelian model of the universe was simple. At the center of the universe was the earth, which Aristotle believed to be round. Surrounding the earth were a series of concentric, crystalline spheres, with the moon, sun, and planets embedded in them. Each of these spheres moved independently, though there were transparent spheres between the planetary spheres that affected the motion of those spheres the way one gear in an automobile transmission affects the other gears. The outermost sphere of Aristotle's cosmos contained the stars—the "fixed stars," as they were known, because they did not move independently, as the planets did. And beyond the fixed stars was . . . nothing. No empty space, no additional spheres. Just . . . nothing.

Although we know today that Aristotle's model of the universe was largely incorrect, there is no denying that it had common sense on its side. Anyone who has ever looked at the sky with the unaided eye on a clear, dark night knows that the planets and stars do seem to be turning about

*Aristotle, the Greek philosopher
and scientific investigator,
developed a comprehensive model
of the universe.*

the earth; they might well have been embedded in clear crystal spheres. And it is easy to assume that heavenly objects must be bound by different laws than the mundane objects on the earth's surface.

Thus, Aristotle's view of the cosmos, originally conceived in the fourth century B.C., reigned supreme well into the sixteenth century A.D., when the Polish astronomer Nicolaus Copernicus revived the theories of Aristarchus and declared that, in fact, the earth was not at the center of the universe. Rather, the sun was at the center of the universe, and the earth and other planets orbited around it. (The moon, however, circled about the earth, just as Aristotle had believed.) Although Copernicus's theory was not widely accepted in the sixteenth century—and we know today that it suffered from a few flaws of its own—it was the first nail in the coffin of the Aristotelian model. The true death knell for Aristotle's theory was sounded a little more than a century later by the seventeenth-century English physicist Isaac Newton, who not only agreed with Copernicus's contention that the planets orbited around the sun, but was able to explain why it was that they did so.

According to a story told by the great physicist himself, the twenty-four-year-old Newton was strolling on his family estate when he saw an apple fall from a tree and wondered if it were pulled to the ground by the same force that held the moon in orbit around the earth. A few calculations later, Newton had his answer. The entire solar system— the earth, the moon, and all of the planets then known—was held together by a single force. And, yes, it was the same force that pulled the apple from the tree, the force called *gravity*.

All matter in the universe produces the attractive force called gravity, though only massive objects such as stars and planets produce enough to have a noticeable effect on other objects, such as apples and moons. On the scale of the solar system, however, it is gravity that shapes the motions of the planets, and this was what Newton realized.

In Newton's universe, all objects tend to remain in motion unless acted on by an outside force, a tendency Aristotle believed to be characteristic only of the heavenly ether. This fact is obscured on the surface of the earth by friction between objects and the ground (or the air), which tends to bring motion to a halt. The planets, on the other hand, move through a nearly frictionless vacuum; in addition, they move in circular motions only because the sun's gravity prevents them from moving in a straight line. Thus, there is no intrinsic difference between, say, a tossed stone (which itself moves in a curved path through the earth's gravitational field) and an orbiting moon; only the specific circumstances are different.

What made Newton's accomplishment so remarkable was that he did not find it necessary to invoke magic to explain the activities of heavenly objects. Rather, he showed that the same rules apply to the planets as apply to earthly apples. The laws are the same in the cosmos as they are on earth. The study of falling apples (or cannonballs

*In the seventeenth century Isaac Newton
provided a new model of the universe.*

or billiard balls) can tell us important things about the universe beyond the reach of our measuring rods. It is possible to understand the heavens in the same rigorous scientific way that we understand things here on earth.

With one giant mental leap, Newton had pushed both physics and cosmology into the modern age. But the picture of the universe available to scientists of Newton's time was still limited. Beyond the orbits of the planets (a few of which in Newton's time had yet to be discovered) lay the "fixed stars," about which almost nothing was known. However, it had been proposed that these flickering points of light were actually distant suns, much like our own sun. But how far away were they? How far did they extend? Was the universe a vast sea of stars, some of them with planets of their own, extending outward to infinity?

The idea that the universe was infinite and filled with solar systems like our own had been proposed even before Newton's birth, most notably by the monk Giordano Bruno in the sixteenth century. Bruno was burned at the stake for uttering such heresies (and for his attacks on orthodox religion). But was the universe really infinite? In the eighteenth century, the Swiss astronomer Jean-Philippe Loys de Cheseaux suggested that if the universe were truly infinite in size, the sky could not be dark at night. Why not? Because if the universe were infinite and uniformly filled with stars, we would see a star at every point in the sky, with no dark space in between. The night sky (and the daytime sky as well) would be as bright as the surface of our sun!

This idea has become known as *Olbers's paradox*, after a nineteenth-century astronomer who revived it. As we will see in a moment, there *are* ways in which the universe could be infinite and the sky still be dark at night, but Olbers's paradox does prove that the universe cannot be infinite, stable, and eternal. In fact, the universe is surprisingly unstable, not at all eternal—and may not even be infinite.

THE FIRST successful attempts to measure the distances to stars were made in the nineteenth century, using methods similar to those of earthbound surveyors who measure distances using trigonometry. Even the nearest stars turned out to be staggeringly far away, at distances measurable in the trillions of miles. So far away are the stars that we usually measure their distances not in miles but in *light-years*—the distance that light, the swiftest entity in the universe, travels in a year. One light-year is roughly equivalent to 6 trillion miles. The nearest star to earth—other than our own sun, of course—is *proxima centauri*, more than four light-years away.

The stars, however, were not the only things that lay beyond the realm of the planets. From the seventeenth century onward, astronomers' telescopes also discerned fuzzy patches of light between the stars. These were generally believed to be clouds of gas floating in space and were therefore dubbed the *nebulae,* from a Greek word meaning "clouds" or "fog." In the eighteenth century, French astronomer Charles Messier began cataloging these objects, a task later continued by his son. Messier was chiefly interested in observing comets; he recorded the positions of the nebulae primarily to warn other comet hunters that these objects were not comets. However, his catalog of the nebulae has proven far more valuable to later generations of astronomers than any of his observations of comets.

Though the majority of astronomers dismissed the nebulae as largely irrelevant to the emerging picture of the universe, a few unusually perceptive individuals suggested that they were the key to understanding the structure of the universe as a whole. In the eighteenth century, a clergyman named Thomas Wright published a book entitled *An Original Theory of the Universe* in which he proposed that the nebulae were made not of gas but of stars, yet were so distant that even through the most powerful telescopes of the time they appeared to be only fuzzy patches of light. Further, Wright argued that our own sun and the nearby stars were all part of just such a cloud of stars, which Wright believed to be spherical in shape. As evidence, Wright pointed to the luminous strip of stars that we see in the night sky, which is known as the Milky Way. The Milky Way, Wright said, was simply the way in which our own nebula appeared to us from our vantage point in its center.

Inspired by a review of Wright's book, the soon-to-be-famous philosopher Immanuel Kant wrote his own book on the subject. Kant suggested that the nebulae were not spherical but disk-shaped. And just as stars tended to group together into nebulae, the nebulae, he said, grouped together into large clusters of nebulae, which in turn grouped into clusters of clusters, and so on and on, in an infinite hierarchy of clusters. In some ways, this is remarkably close to the way we view the structure of the universe today, though Kant carried the idea a bit too far.

Although the idea that the nebulae were "island universes" enjoyed a certain vogue in the eighteenth century, it was never taken seriously by the majority of astronomers. And it was not until the 1920s that powerful enough telescopes were built to allow the issue to be resolved once and for all. By this time it had become obvious that we did indeed live inside a disklike cluster of stars (though the American astronomer Harlow Shapley had shown that we were not at its center but about two-thirds of the way toward its edge). This disk-shaped cloud of stars had come to be called the *galaxy* (from a Greek word meaning, literally, "milky way"). However, it was by no means ob-

The Milky Way galaxy—from Sagittarius to Cassiopeia—stretches down the length of a mosaic photograph.

vious that the nebulae were also galaxies, separate from our own. Shapley and others did not believe that they were; they believed that our own galaxy represented the entirety of the universe. What lay beyond our galaxy? No one was sure, but obviously it was not stars. This neatly resolved the problem of the dark night sky. If the realm of the stars was not infinite, then Olbers's paradox was no longer paradoxical.

The only clue that Shapley might be wrong came in the form of supernovas, bright stellar explosions visible across vast reaches of space. Certain of the larger nebulae, such as the one dubbed M31 in Andromeda—that is, object number 31 in Messier's catalog, found in the constellation of Andromeda—were the scene of an unusually large number of these explosions. Although Shapley argued that these explosions were unrelated to the nebulae, it seemed to other astronomers that this was too improbable a coincidence and that the supernovas must be *within* the nebulae. That is, they must represent explosions among the stars that make up the nebulae themselves.

The issue was finally settled in 1924. Using the new 100-inch telescope at Mount Wilson—the largest telescope available at the time—the American astronomer Edwin Hubble succeeded in

Edwin Hubble, at Mt. Wilson Observatory in California, developed ways to study nebulae.

photographing individual stars within the Andromeda nebula, proving that it was indeed a vast cloud of stars. But was this cloud of stars inside our own galaxy, or was it a separate galaxy in its own right? To answer this question, it was necessary for Hubble to measure the distance from earth to these stars.

This was a tricky proposition, because the surveying techniques that nineteenth-century astronomers had used to measure the distances to nearby stars were worthless at such vast distances. Instead, Hubble measured the distance to the Andromeda nebula by timing the cycles of *cepheid variables.*

The cepheids had been discovered several years earlier by American astronomer Henrietta Swan Leavitt. They are stars that change brightness over a period of hours, days, or weeks. Further, there is a relationship between the amount of time that it takes a cepheid to go through a complete cycle of change and the amount of light that the cepheid produces during that cycle. If you know how long it takes a cepheid to complete a cycle, then you can calculate how bright the cepheid is at the brightest (or dimmest) point in that cycle.

How did this help Edwin Hubble measure the distance to the Andromeda nebula? It is possible to measure the distance to a star based on how bright the star appears to be when viewed from earth. Like anything else that produces light, from streetlamps to automobile headlights, a star appears brighter when viewed close up than when viewed far away. Since there is a strict mathematical relationship between distance and apparent brightness (the brightness that the star *appears* to have when viewed from earth), we can calculate how far away it is. But first we must know how bright the star *actually* is, that is, how bright it would appear to be if viewed from a relatively nearby position. A star that appears to be bright when viewed from earth may be a relatively bright star that is quite far away or a relatively dim star that is unusually close by.

Ordinarily, there is no way to know how bright a distant star actually is and so there is no way to calculate its distance based on brightness. Cepheids, however, provide a way to determine the brightness of a star based on something that does not depend on distance—the timing of its cycle of changing brightness—and thus cepheids can be used for determining interstellar distances. After months of searching, Hubble found several cepheids in the Andromeda nebula, timed their cycles, and thereby determined their distance. Since the cepheids were part of the nebula, this was also the distance to the nebula itself, and it was indeed greater than the distance to any stars within our own galaxy. The Andromeda nebula became the Andromeda galaxy.

Although not all nebulae turned out to be galaxies—some were, in fact, clouds of gas after all—most of them did indeed turn out to be "island universes" separate from our own galaxy. We now know that there are roughly as many galaxies in the observable universe—about 100 billion of them—as there are stars in our own galaxy. It is the galaxy, not the star, that is the primary building block of the universe.

Thanks to Edwin Hubble (and the astronomers who refined his distance measurements in succeeding decades), we now know that the Andromeda galaxy is about 2 million light-years away, a distance very hard for the human mind to comprehend. (For that matter, the distance to even the nearest stars is very hard for the human mind to comprehend.) The Andromeda galaxy, furthermore, is relatively nearby as galaxies go. Most galaxies are even farther away, some at distances measurable in the billions of light-years. And still others must lie far beyond the reach of our telescopes, perhaps beyond the limits of any telescopes that will ever be built.

And yet the vast size of the universe was not the major cosmological discovery of the twentieth century. Even as Edwin Hubble measured the distance to several other nearby galaxies, he made another discovery that cast light on the very birth of the universe itself.

IN THE YEAR 1917, the German-born American physicist Albert Einstein published his General Theory of Relativity. Like his earlier Special Theory of Relativity, best remembered by nonscientists for its startling assertion that time and space are so closely interwoven that our perception of time changes according to our motion through space, the General Theory profoundly altered the way in which scientists look at the universe.

Einstein, in the General Theory, tackled a subject that had overwhelmed even the great Isaac Newton: the nature of gravity. Newton had understood how gravity worked, of course, and had been able to describe the structure of the solar system in terms of gravitational attraction. But he had been unable to explain just why gravity was able to reach out over great distances, invisibly, and influence the motion of planets. Picking up where Newton left off, Einstein was able to show that the "force" of gravity was actually brought about by a kind of curvature in space. In the vicinity of large objects, space was "warped," and this curvature influenced the motion of objects moving through this space. Thus, the orbiting planets are actually rolling around the edge of a "hole" in space produced by the mass of the sun.

How can space be curved? This is a difficult concept to visualize, though it can be expressed quite clearly in mathematical terms. The way in which space is affected by the mass of stars and planets can be compared to the depression that a cannonball might make if placed on a stretched rubber sheet, though the analogy is not very exact. Just as the depression in the rubber would cause a rolling marble to veer toward the cannonball, so small objects in space are attracted to larger objects.

So great is the collective mass of all the matter in the universe that this curvature of space is one of the dominant characteristics of our universe when

viewed on a cosmic level. Just how great is that mass we will see in the next chapter.

While Einstein was working out his description of the universe in terms of curved space-time (space and time having been united into a single entity by the Special Theory), he was troubled by a recurring problem. The universe he constructed tended, quite literally, to collapse. This was a problem that had also troubled Newton, who had speculated that in a finite universe—a universe that did not go on forever—the gravity of the stars and planets would have caused all the matter in the universe to drift together into a large clump in the center. Newton had solved this problem by assuming that the universe was infinitely large and had no center. In the curved universe of Einstein, however, this solution no longer worked.

To prevent his constructed universe from collapsing under its own gravitational pull, Einstein assumed the existence of a universal expansive force, which tended to push everything apart. We've never noticed this force, Einstein suggested, because it grows greater with distance. It would only operate on the large scale of the universe, not on the small scale of our solar system.

Alas, when Einstein added this expansive force to his model of the universe, it became unsta-

Albert Einstein's work in theoretical physics transformed the way scientists view the universe.

ble. It tended to expand, quite explosively, at the slightest excuse. In frustration, Einstein added a new term to his equations which he called the *cosmological constant,* for the sole purpose of keeping the universe steady. But when others began to play with Einstein's equations, most notably the Russian cosmologist Alexander Friedmann, they discovered that not even the cosmological constant was enough to keep it from expanding. Despite this, Einstein denounced any speculation that his theories showed the universe to be expanding; wasn't it obvious that the universe was as stable as a rock?

Well, no. Even as cosmologists bickered about the implications of Einstein's theories, Edwin Hubble was patiently measuring the distances to other galaxies. Not only did he measure their distances, but he measured the velocities with which those galaxies were moving relative to our own, and it was these measurements that upset prevailing ideas about the stability of the universe.

How could Hubble measure the velocity of something as distant as a galaxy? The key to such measurements is the *Doppler effect,* discovered in the nineteenth century by Austrian physicist Christian Doppler. Doppler noted that the pitch of a sound wave changed if the object producing the sound changed velocity relative to the person listening to the sound. If the sound-producing object—a fire engine, say—is moving toward you, the sound becomes higher pitched. If it is moving away from you, it becomes lower pitched. The reason, as Doppler recognized, is that the sound waves become, in effect, bunched together in front of the object moving toward you and stretched out in the wake of the object moving away from you. This changes the wavelength (and therefore the pitch) of the sound waves.

Something similar happens to the light of a galaxy as it moves toward or away from the earth. In the case of a galaxy moving toward the earth, the light waves become bunched together and are therefore shifted toward the blue end of the color spectrum; we refer to this effect as a *blue shift*. In the case of a galaxy moving away from the earth, the light waves become stretched out and therefore are shifted toward the red end of the spectrum; we refer to this effect as a *red shift*. (This effect can only be detected when the light from the galaxy is analyzed by a spectrograph. The visible color of the light does not actually change.)

When Hubble examined the light of distant galaxies—i.e., those too far away to be affected by the gravity of our own—he found that they all displayed a red shift, without exception. Further, the more distant a galaxy is from the earth, the more severely red-shifted is its light. Almost certainly, Hubble reasoned, this meant that these galaxies were speeding away from our galaxy—and from each other. The universe was indeed expanding, just as Einstein's theory had suggested.

In 1927, Belgian astronomer Abbe Georges Lemaitres drew the obvious conclusion that, if all the galaxies are moving rapidly apart from one another today, they must all have been much closer together in the past. In fact, there must have been a time when all of the matter in the universe was crushed together into a single, ultradense mass, which Lemaitres called the *cosmic egg*. This "egg" must have been blown apart by a gigantic explosion, which led to the expanding universe that we see today. In 1950, British astronomer Fred Hoyle gave this explosion its colloquial name: the *Big Bang*. Hoyle was an advocate of a very different cosmological theory, the so-called *steady-state theory*, and had intended the phrase "Big Bang" as a term of derision; he was making fun of the theory. But the name Big Bang stuck, and we still use it today. Even Fred Hoyle has subsequently come to accept the theory, although reluctantly.

The main objection that astronomers such as Hoyle voiced against the Big Bang theory was that there was no way scientists could either prove or disprove it. If the universe was actually born in a cosmic explosion, that explosion would have taken place in the distant past, and there is no evidence of it that can be observed today. In effect, Hoyle was saying that it was necessary for scientists to invoke magic to explain the origin of the universe, as the ancient astronomers had done to explain the current state of the cosmos. Because there was no direct evidence for the birth of the universe, or experiments that would prove how it was born, we would forever be unable to explain this "Big Bang" in terms of the natural laws that govern the universe today.

As it turned out, Hoyle was wrong.

After World War II, new forms of astronomy arose that allowed scientists to study types of radiation from space other than visible light, including X rays, gamma rays, and radio waves. In 1966, two physicists in the employ of the Bell Telephone Company, Arno Penzias and Robert Wilson, were given the use of an antenna originally used for receiving signals from communications satellites. While working to prepare the antenna for use in radio-wave astronomy, Penzias and Wilson were annoyed to find that they were receiving a strange radio hum in their antenna that seemed to come from all parts of the sky. Even cleaning the pigeon droppings (which they later referred to delicately as "a white dielectric substance") out of the antenna didn't remove the hum.

Finally, they mentioned the problem to an astronomer, who referred them to physicist Robert Dicke of Princeton University. Dicke knew quite well what the hum was that Penzias and Wilson were receiving. It was the microwave "echo" left over from the Big Bang itself. He and his colleagues had just theorized the existence of such an echo and had not yet gotten around to looking for it.

This was astonishing news. The idea that the universe was born in a huge explosion was now confirmed, and scientists could actually begin to study that explosion in some detail. It was no longer necessary to invoke quasi-magical explanations; the origin of the universe could now be explained using the ordinary tools of scientific

*Robert Wilson (left) and Arno Penzias
—working with a Bell Laboratories
antenna—discovered the "microwave
echo" left over from the Big Bang.*

explanation. The *cosmic microwave background radiation* discovered by Penzias and Wilson led to another kind of explosion, an explosion of fresh knowledge about the birth of the universe. Within the next two decades, cosmological science was virtually born again. New-theories of the origin of the universe gushed forth, each more incredible— and yet more firmly grounded in observed facts— than the last.

In the chapters that follow, we'll acquaint you not only with these new theories of the Big Bang, but also with the new ideas in both physics and astronomy that have made these theories possible.

THE COSMOS
TODAY

According to most theories, it has been roughly 18 billion (give or take a few billion) years since the Big Bang. Before we take a look at the universe in that distant past, though, let's take a closer look at the universe in the present.

The most important part of the universe to human beings in general is, obviously, the planet we live on. The earth is one of nine planets circling around a star that we usually refer to, simply, as the sun. (To distinguish our sun from other stars, we sometimes refer to it by the Latin name *sol*, from which we get the adjective *solar.*)

The second most important part of the universe, from the point of view of virtually all living organisms on our planet, is that very same sun. It provides almost all of the energy necessary for living creatures to exist. It is the energy of the sun, for instance, that allows plants to manufacture carbohydrates through photosynthesis, and these carbohydrates, in turn, are the ultimate source of the food eaten by animals. It is the sun that makes the rivers flow, by evaporating water in lowland regions and moving it back to the highlands, so that it can flow downhill again and generate hydroelectric power for our use. It is the sun that makes the wind blow so that windmills can turn and sailboats sail. It is the sun that made plants grow in ancient times so that they could be buried underground for millions of years and produce the oil and coal and natural gas that we use today to fuel our cars and factories.

In a sense, the earth and sun are the only parts of the universe that are of pressing interest to human beings. If the rest of the universe were to softly and silently vanish away, most human beings would little care or notice. On a typical smoggy suburban night, it might be hard to tell the difference.

And yet this earth-sun system that is so important to human beings is only the smallest, most infinitesimal fraction of the vast universe in which we live. Even taking our entire solar system into account, with its nine known planets, uncounted asteroids and comets, and of course the sun, we are still far less significant to the universe as a whole than a tiny dot of ink would be to a world map that covered an entire wall of an auditorium.

Our sun, for instance, is but one of 100 billion stars that make up the Milky Way galaxy. As stars go, it is average, neither unusually bright nor unusually dim. It has a predicted lifetime of about 10

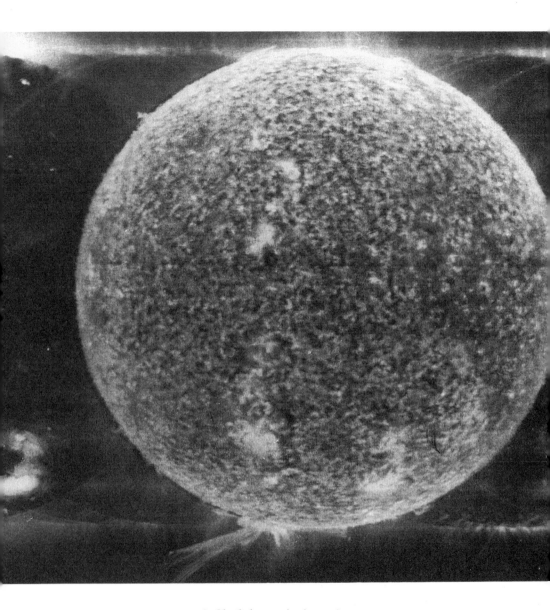

*A Skylab 2 mission, in 1973,
provided a close-up view of the sun.*

billion years, about half of which has already passed. At the end of this time, it will begin to die what is, by stellar standards, an unspectacular death. For a brief period, perhaps another billion years at most, it will expand into a bloated red giant, a dull red star many times larger than the sun is now. Then it will collapse like a pricked balloon, deflating until it is only a few dozen miles in diameter, becoming an extremely dense star of a type we call a *white dwarf*. A spoonful of matter in the white dwarf would weigh a ton. It will remain hot and glowing for billions of years, then will cool off to become a *black dwarf.*

The majority of stars will die a similar death. However, unusually large and massive stars will meet a more spectacular demise. Violent nuclear reactions in their cores will cause them to explode in vivid supernovas, which will be so bright that they will be visible to observers in distant galaxies. They will then collapse far more violently than our sun will, becoming *neutron stars*, or even *black holes*, so compact that they are unable to stop shrinking. The gravity produced by a black hole is so intense that even light cannot escape from it; hence its name. In terms of Einstein's General Theory of Relativity, we say that the black hole has produced such a deep, extremely curved hole in the fabric of space-time that it has vanished from the universe completely. All of these strange, dense objects—white dwarfs, neutron stars, and black holes—are a part of the universe around us.

Between the stars is a nearly continuous cloud of gas and dust called the *interstellar medium*. Although not thick enough to be considered an atmosphere—in fact, it is so thin that we on earth might consider it to be a total vacuum, were we exposed to it—it is nonetheless a very real part of the universe between the stars. It is made mostly of the gas hydrogen, far and away the most common element in the universe. When astronomers take photographs of stars, this interstellar medium colors their photographs like a dingy yellow haze. In places, the interstellar medium thickens up considerably, so that it looks like a cloud hanging in space. These thickenings of the interstellar medium are the true nebulae, the ones described in the last chapter that did not turn out to be distant galaxies.

Sometimes one of these nebulae, perhaps buffeted by the shock waves from a nearby supernova, becomes unusually thick and begins to collapse under the gravitational attraction of the tiny particles of dust and gas that make it up. Friction between these particles heats the cloud until it glows, eventually triggering a process called *hydrogen fusion* that causes the cloud to explode like a gigantic hydrogen bomb. Such an explosion, contained by its own gravity, can continue for millions or even billions of years. We call such an explosion a star. Our own sun began as just such an interstellar cloud, 5 billion years ago.

When astronomers train their telescopes on the heavens, they can see stars, nebulae, the interstellar medium, and even dim white dwarfs and neutron stars. (By definition, they cannot see black holes, though X-ray telescopes have detected bursts of powerful radiation that may be produced by matter trapped in a black hole's powerful gravitational field.)

It is tempting to think that this is all there is to the universe, a vast and endless sea of stars, nebulae, collapsed stars, and other objects, stretching away neatly to infinity. As we saw in the last chapter, however, this is not so. The matter in space has a tendency to clump together into the aggregates that we call galaxies. Our own sun and all stars visible to the naked eye are part of the Milky Way galaxy. There are roughly 100 billion stars in the Milky Way galaxy. Shaped like a gigantic disk, the Milky Way stretches about 100,000 light-years from one end to the other.

Through our telescopes we can see literally billions of other galaxies. Some of these are disk-shaped (and most display a distinct spiral pattern when viewed through a powerful telescope, as would our own galaxy if we could see it from the outside) and others are elliptical; still others are irregular in shape, like scattered clouds blown ahead of a storm.

Just as stars group together into galaxies, the galaxies tend to group together into galactic clusters. And there is considerable evidence that these galactic clusters group together into clusters of clusters, or *superclusters*. Immanuel Kant would have nodded his head sagely at this "modern"

revelation. But unlike Kant's vision of infinite levels of clusters within clusters, the galactic clustering that astronomers observe in the universe seems to stop at the supercluster level. The superclusters really do seem to be spread evenly throughout the universe. If we could step outside the universe and study it from such a distance that each supercluster were a mere pinpoint of light, the universe would seem remarkably smooth and even.

This might not seem like a terribly important fact, but cosmologists find it more than a little surprising. Given what we are now learning about the creation of the universe in the Big Bang, there is no reason to suppose that the universe should be smooth and even throughout. It would make more sense to suppose that the universe might be a jumbled mess, with some parts filled with a thin gas of hydrogen and no stars whatsoever, some parts filled with stars but no galaxies, some parts filled with galaxies but no galactic clusters, and so forth. And yet the universe is uniformly filled with galactic superclusters.

The cosmic background radiation discovered by Penzias and Wilson verifies the remarkable smoothness of the universe. No matter what part

The Andromeda galaxy is one of approximately 100 billion galaxies in the observable universe.

of the sky we point our radio telescopes toward, this radiation left over from the Big Bang—or, more accurately, from a period shortly after the Big Bang—is exactly the same. The smoothness and evenness of this radiation reflects the smoothness and evenness of the universe. Why should the universe be so smooth?

We can compare the smoothness of the universe to a bathtub that has just been filled with water. As the water flows into the tub, it is at first cold (because the hot water from the water heater has not yet reached the tap), then it becomes progressively warmer. As the tub fills and the hot water from the tap moves into the far end of the tub, it loses some of its heat to the air. Thus, different parts of the water in the tub will be at different temperatures, with the part nearest to the tap warmest and the part farthest from the tap coolest.

Yet once the tub is filled, the temperature of the water will gradually change until it is almost exactly the same throughout. This occurs because the hot, fast-moving molecules of water will speed around the tub, bumping into colder, slow-moving molecules, thus losing some of their heat to the cold molecules. Eventually, all of the molecules of water, from one end of the tub to the other, will be moving at more or less the same speed—on average, anyway—and will therefore have roughly the same temperature.

Note, however, that this process takes time. The hot molecules must first travel across the tub, carrying their heat with them, before all the water in the tub is at the same temperature. The same thing would have been true of the early universe, shortly after the Big Bang. There is no particular reason that all parts of the universe should have been at the same temperature or that exactly the same structures should have been forming at the same moment all over the universe. With sufficient time, particles from one part of the newborn universe could have spread throughout the universe, bringing the entire universe to roughly the same temperature, thus making it as smooth as we see it today. (And, yes, we can speak of the universe as having a temperature, which we define simply as the average motion of the tiny particles that make up the universe.) But, if the universe has always been expanding at the same rate that it is expanding today, there has not been enough time since the Big Bang for any particle to reach the end of the universe. (Bear in mind that Einstein's Special Theory of Relativity tells us that no particle can move faster than the speed of light.) So why is the universe so smooth and even throughout? We'll come back to this question in Chapter Six.

PERHAPS THE FIRST question that any child asks about the universe, as soon as he or she becomes aware that anything exists beyond the earth, is: How big is the universe? It is actually possible to offer a tentative answer to this question. But before we can attempt such an answer, we must first ask a second, related question: What shape is the universe?

How can the universe have a shape? In the last chapter, we saw how Einstein's General Theory of Relativity described the curvature of space. Just as a string or a piece of paper can be curved, so can space itself be curved. It is difficult to visualize such a curve in our heads because we have no sensory organs with which to directly identify curved space the way that we can identify curved paper or string. Nonetheless, space *can* become curved.

When Alexander Friedmann worked with Einstein's equations in the early 1920s, he showed that the mass of all the matter in the universe is sufficient to give the universe itself a shape. The exact shape of the universe depends on just how much matter there is in the universe—or, to be more precise, on just how densely packed together the matter in the universe is. According to Friedmann, there are three possible shapes that the universe could have. He called them *closed, open,* and *flat.*

We can compare a closed universe to a sphere or globe. Like a sphere, the closed universe would be so severely curved that it would actually close back in on itself. A space traveler who set outward in a straight line through a closed universe would eventually return to his or her starting point, even though he or she had never turned around. (Of course, the trip would take many billions of years to finish, even at the speed of light.) This is similar to the way in which a traveler on the surface of the earth can travel continuously east (or west or north or south) and eventually return to the point at which he or she started. In effect, our imaginary space traveler would circumnavigate the universe.

An open universe, on the other hand, can be compared to a saddle, but a saddle that stretches outward infinitely without an edge. Technically, the shape of the open universe is known as a *hyperbola*. A space traveler who set outward into an open universe could never return to his or her starting point without first turning around.

A flat universe is right on the edge between the closed and the open universe. A space traveler who set outward into a closed universe would eventually return to where he or she started, but only after an infinite amount of time had passed. A flat universe can be compared to an infinitely large tabletop.

If the universe is open, then the answer to the question *how big is it?* is quite simple. It is infinitely big. The universe goes on forever. It has no edge, no end. Is it filled with an infinite number of stars, galaxies, and clusters of galaxies? We have no way of knowing for sure, but lacking evidence to the contrary, we have to assume that it is.

You might ask how the universe can be infinitely large without violating Olbers's paradox, mentioned in the last chapter. If the universe is infinitely large, and filled with an infinite number of stars, then the sky should be blazing with starlight. Yet it is not.

The answer is that, while the universe may well be infinitely large, we now know that it is not infinitely old; rather, it has been around for about 18 billion years, give or take a few billion. The light that we see from the stars in the sky has traveled toward us at a finite speed, the speed of light. Much of that light has taken thousands, millions, even billions of years to get here. We cannot see any stars or galaxies more than 18 billion light-years away. Therefore, the universe must be only 18 billion years old. If there are stars further away, they are invisible to us. And that is why the sky is not filled with a blinding blaze of starlight.

If the universe is closed, on the other hand, then it would have a finite size. We would actually be able to give a specific figure, in light-years, for the circumference of the universe. (The circumference of the universe is the distance that our hypothetical space traveler would have to travel outward in order to return to the point from which he or she started.) According to physicist-cosmologist Steven Weinberg, in his classic book about the Big Bang entitled *The First Three Minutes*, a small closed universe might now have a circumference of about 125 billion light-years.[1] Of course, this is merely a guess and may be wildly wrong; further, it should be borne in mind that this figure changes with time. Because the universe is expanding, it would have been smaller in the past and will be larger in the future.

This is true, of course, only for a closed universe. If the universe is infinite, then it would always have been infinite and will always be infinite. We cannot properly speak of something infi-

nitely large as changing in size. We can only say that it becomes more or less dense as the matter it contains comes closer together or moves farther apart.

Is there any way that we can tell whether the universe is open, closed, or flat? Surprisingly, there is. As we said before, it is the amount of matter in the universe (and the gravity that the matter produces) that makes the difference between an open and a closed universe. Although we can't count all of the individual bits of matter in the universe to see if there are enough to make the universe closed—in fact, we can't even *see* all of the matter in the universe, since the light from most of it has not reached us yet—it is nonetheless possible to make this calculation based on the *density* of matter in the observable portion of the universe. If we look at the matter spread out over a large portion of the universe, and average it out as though it were spread evenly over that portion, then the universe will be closed if the average density is greater than three atoms of matter per cubic meter of space. If the density is less than this, the universe will be open. If the density is *exactly* three atoms of matter per cubic meter, then the universe will be flat.

Three atoms per cubic meter of space doesn't sound very dense. (We'll have more to say about atoms in the next chapter; for now, suffice it to say that they are extremely small.) And yet, as astronomers search the skies with their various kinds of telescopes—optical telescopes, radio telescopes,

X-ray telescopes, gamma-ray telescopes, etc.—they can't even find this much matter. They can only find about 1/100th of the amount of matter necessary to make the universe closed, or about three atoms for every *hundred* cubic meters of space.

And yet it is possible, perhaps even probable, that there is a lot of matter in the universe that is not visible to astronomers. This is sometimes called the *missing mass* or *invisible matter.*

Where might this missing mass be? One possible place is inside black holes. When a black hole forms, the entire mass of the star disappears inside it. Further, a large black hole can swallow any objects that enter its vicinity, including other stars. There is even evidence that the centers of some galaxies (including, perhaps, our own) are being absorbed into the voracious maws of a black hole. Matter inside a black hole would be invisible as far as astronomers were concerned, and might represent additional mass toward the amount necessary to close the universe. However, it is doubtful that there is a hundred times as much mass in black holes as outside of them.

A more likely location for the missing mass is in so-called *galactic halos.* Just as the planets in our solar system revolve around the sun, so the stars in a galaxy revolve around the galactic center, held in place by the collective mass of the other stars in the galaxy. However, telescopic examination of the way in which spiral galaxies such as our own rotate indicates that they are rotating much too rapidly to

*The stars in the Milky Way galaxy
revolve around a galactic center,
forming a delicate spiral.*

be stable. They should fly apart like an out-of-control merry-go-round, or at least lose their delicate spiral form, after a few turns. And yet all indications are that these galaxies have been spinning in much their present form for billions of years.

Studies of the way in which the matter in a galaxy behaves gravitationally indicate that these galaxies are surrounded by vast halos of invisible matter, as though the glowing, visible part of the galaxy were only the cream filling in the pastry, as it were. But why can't we see the material in this halo? Because it can only interact with other matter gravitationally. It does not produce or interact with light rays or any other kind of radiation. Hence, it is invisible to us. We see right through it.

If this is true, then perhaps 90 percent of the matter in the universe may be invisible, and thus the universe will have 91 percent of the matter that it needs to be closed. Though this still isn't enough, it is possible that the remaining 9 percent or so may be in tiny particles known as *neutrinos*, which scientists have long believed to have no mass at all. Neutrinos are so abundant that even if they turned out to have an infinitesimal amount of mass, it might be enough to make the universe closed.

As we will see in Chapter Seven, this question of whether the universe is open or closed affects more than just its shape. The question and its answer can lead us to some very important ideas about the universe's long-term future.

Even if the universe has only 1 percent of the matter needed to make it closed (or flat), this is surprisingly close to the amount that is actually needed. If you don't agree, consider that there is nothing that says the universe couldn't have had only one ten-millionth of the mass density required to make it closed, or even 20 billion times too much. The actual mass density seems to be remarkably close to the amount required for perfect flatness, within a factor of one hundred, and there are indications that the amount is even closer to the flatness figure than we realize. Isn't this a bit of a coincidence? Such coincidences bother scientists, and so they have given a great deal of thought to this question. In Chapter Seven, we will offer a possible answer.

LOOKED AT on the large scale, the universe is a place of staggering immensity and fascinating variety, filled as it is with nebulae and black holes, dark matter and exploding stars, and other things that we haven't mentioned here. And yet, roughly 18 billion years ago, the universe might have been much smaller than it is now—or at least, the matter in the universe must have been packed a great deal more densely than it is now.

As a result, there were no stars or galaxies or nebulae or black holes or planets in the universe right after the Big Bang. There weren't even atoms, the very constituents of matter itself. The universe in the moments immediately after the Big Bang was so very different from the universe that we see today that in order to understand what it was like, we must first take a look at how our world appears on a very different scale, the scale of the extremely small. We must go from the macrocosm to the microcosm, from the world of the very large to the world of the very small, to take a look at the particles that make up matter—and, in some cases, the particles that make up the particles.

THREE

THE MICROCOSMOS

When you go to a different country, you expect things to be done in a different way. Automobiles may be driven on the "wrong" side of the road; food may be eaten with different utensils; social customs may be precisely opposite to those you are accustomed to.

In the country of the very small—the land of the minute particles that make up ordinary matter—things are very different than they are in the country of the relatively large, i.e., the land where we live out our everyday lives. The study of this world of infinitesimally small particles is called *quantum mechanics.* When you first study quantum mechanics (when *anybody* first studies quantum mechanics) there is a temptation to wonder if the physicists who dreamed it up have gone completely crazy. The land of the infinitesimally small is, to put it mildly, rather weird.

In the land of the relatively large, we are used to thinking of objects as having definite locations in time and space, of certain events always being followed by other events, of solid objects being constructed from other solid objects. In the world of quantum mechanics, on the other hand, the location of an object can become fuzzy, events only have *probabilities* of being followed by other events, and the particles that make up solid matter are not solid at all.

The English language, alas, was designed for describing the land of the relatively large, not the quantum world. There are no words for much of what occurs among the fundamental particles of matter. Thus, it is necessary to describe such events through the use of metaphor, i.e., by comparing them to events with which we are familiar. Unfortunately, in many cases there *are* no familiar events with which quantum mechanical events can be accurately compared, and thus our metaphors are likely to be imprecise. All metaphorical descriptions of quantum events, including those in this chapter, should be taken as the closest approximation we can make of these events.

In this book, we will frequently use the word "particle" to describe the components of matter. This word is deceptive. It is tempting to think of these fundamental particles as being like particles of sand or miniature billiard balls. They are not. They are like nothing that you have experienced in the world of the relatively large. Perhaps it would be better if we used the term "entities"—as in *subatomic entities* or *fundamental entities*—rather than the word "particles." Unfortunately, the word "particles" has become so firmly entrenched in the language of physics that it cannot be avoided, and it would be foolish even to try. However, you should bear in mind that the particles to which we refer in the rest of this book are nothing like the particles with which you are familiar in the everyday world.

It is best to come to a description of the quantum world without preconceptions. Thus, we will organize our description of quantum mechanics in this chapter as a series of Amazing Facts, to emphasize the fact that much of this information goes against our normal conception of the way things work.

You may already be aware of some of these "amazing facts" from other books that you've read, but they never really lose their capacity to amaze. The quantum world is strange indeed.

Amazing Fact Number 1
All matter is made up of particles.

The idea that so-called solid matter is actually made up of tiny entities known as atoms is not new; it was first proposed by the ancient Greeks. Nearly two hundred years ago, the English chemist John Dalton worked out a comprehensive description of all known types of matter as being made up of less than one hundred different kinds of atoms, which he called the *elements*. This represented a tremendous advance in the way that scientists viewed the ultimate nature of the universe, though it was not widely accepted in Dalton's time.

In the twentieth century, however, it was discovered that atoms were in turn made up of even smaller particles, which we refer to collectively as *subatomic particles.* In fact, all of the different types of atoms are made up of only three different kinds of particles: the *proton*, the *electron*, and the *neutron*. Just as Dalton's theory represented a substantial simplification of the way in which scientists had previously viewed the nature of matter, so the discovery of subatomic particles greatly simplified Dalton's theory.

Doubtless you have seen drawings of the structure of atoms. The protons and the neutrons clump together in a roughly spherical conglomeration in the center of the atom, which is known as the *nucleus.* (For this reason, we sometimes refer to protons and neutrons collectively as *nucleons.*) The electrons orbit around the nucleus like tiny planets. This is a simplification of what actually takes place inside an atom, one of those tricky metaphors that we mentioned earlier, but it will do as a first approximation of atomic structure.

The particles that make up the atom, however, are not the only existing subatomic particles. In fact, they are but a few out of several hundred particles that physicists have "observed" with the aid of special viewing instruments called *particle accelerators*, also known as *atom smashers, super-colliders, sychrotrons,* and so on.

The Fermi National Accelerator Laboratory, in Illinois, is a center for research exploring the basic structure of matter.

We can distinguish one particle from another only by the *properties* of the particles. One of the properties that particles have is *mass*, which, among other things, determines how heavy the particle is when it comes within a gravitational field, such as the gravitational field of earth. It is the sum total of the mass of the particles that make up an object that determines how much mass the object has. And it is mass that determines how heavy the object will be, say, on the surface of the earth. For instance, if you weigh 120 pounds (54 kg), then the mass of all the particles that make up your body must add up to 120 pounds. On the surface of the earth, this means that you weigh 120 pounds, though you would weigh less, say, on the moon. In space, far from any strong gravitational fields, you would weigh almost nothing at all, but you would still have 120 pounds of mass.

Mass, however, is not the only property that distinguishes one particle from another. Another property found in many particles is *electric charge.* This property comes in two varieties: negative and positive. A charged particle will be either negatively charged or positively charged. (Some particles are not charged at all.)

What is electric charge? No one knows precisely, but we can identify electric charge by the way in which charged particles interact with one another. Two negatively charged particles will repel one another, that is, push one another away. Similarly, two positively charged particles will also repel one another. Thus, we say that *like charges repel*. On the other hand, a negatively charged particle will attract a positively charged particle and vice versa. Thus, we say that *opposite charges attract*.

The protons in the nucleus of the atom are positively charged. The electrons orbiting the nucleus are negatively charged. It is the attraction between the electrons and the protons that prevents the electrons from flying away from the nucleus, in a fashion similar (but not identical) to the way in which the sun's gravity prevents the planets of the solar system from flying away into the depths of space.

Another property possessed by subatomic particles is *spin*, which can be viewed as being something like the spin of a top or the rotation of a planet on its axis. This analogy is not very precise—particles do not spin in quite the same way as tops and planets do—but there are similarities. Other properties of subatomic particles have such bizarre names as *color, strangeness, charm, truth,* and *beauty*. These names are largely whimsical; the particles don't really have color in the visual sense or anything analogous to truth or beauty. Nonetheless, scientists use these names to identify, distinguish between, and explain the interactions of certain subatomic particles.

In a sense, these properties are all there is to a particle. That is, it is inaccurate to think of a particle as some kind of tiny object that possesses properties such as charge and spin the way that a rubber ball might possess the property of bounciness. Rather, the properties *are* the particle—or at least they are the only part of the particle that physicists can detect with their instruments, and so they might as well be all that there is to the particle. It is dangerous, though, to fall into the trap of thinking of the particle as being a real, solid object that spins, produces electric charges, and so forth, because pretty soon you'll start running up against logical contradictions, as we'll see in the next few pages. Better to think of the particle as having no existence at all, aside from these properties. The properties are all that there is to the particle. Period.

Amazing Fact Number 2
Particles interact through forces.

If particles were all there were in the universe, then the universe would be a pretty dull place. Nothing would ever happen in it. Most of the interesting things going on around us are the result of *interactions* between particles, that is, the way in which particles influence each other. These interactions take the form of *forces*.

We saw an example of one such force in the first Amazing Fact. A pair of charged particles will either repel or attract one another, depending on whether they carry the same or opposite electric charges. This repulsion or attraction is called the *electromagnetic force*.

It is the electromagnetic force that holds the electrons in orbit around the nucleus of the atom. It is also the electromagnetic force that holds atoms together in what we call *molecules*. And it is the electromagnetic force that causes molecules of matter to stick together to form larger objects, such as books and people.

Gravity, which we met in the previous chapters, is also a force. It is gravity that holds very large clumps of matter, such as planets and stars, together. And it is gravity that holds solar systems, galaxies, and clusters of galaxies together.

Surprisingly, gravity is much weaker than the electromagnetic force. The reason that we rarely notice the effect of the electromagnetic force in our everyday lives is that most objects contain equal amounts of positive and negative electric charges. The two types of charges cancel one another out, so that most objects have no overall charge, and thus large objects do not tend to attract or repel one another electromagnetically the way that subatomic particles do. In fact, because atoms are generally composed of equal numbers of positively charged protons and negatively charged electrons, few have any electric charge at all. (Sometimes, however, an atom can lose one or more of its electrons and gain an overall positive charge. Such a charged atom is called an *ion.*)

Gravity, as far as we know, comes in only one variety. Although a single particle of matter produces only the tiniest amount of gravity, much smaller than the amount of electromagnetic force produced by, say, an electron, a very large mass of particles (such as a planet or star) will produce an amount of gravity equal to the combined gravity of all its particles. Thus, gravity is cumulative. On the scale of a solar system or a galaxy, it is gravity that is the most obvious force holding things together. On the scale of an atom or a molecule, on the other hand, electromagnetism is vastly more powerful.

It is not the most powerful force, however. If it were, the atomic nucleus could not exist. You'll recall that the nucleus of an atom is made of protons and neutrons. Protons have a positive electric charge. Neutrons, as their name implies, have no charge at all (that is, they are electrically neutral). If like charges repel, then the protons in the nucleus should repel one another—and yet they don't. We can guess from this that there must be a force holding the nucleus together that is even stronger than the electromagnetic force. And, in fact, there is. We refer to this force—appropriately—as the *strong force*. Objects that produce the strong force always attract one another; they never repel. It is the strong force that holds the nucleus together.

The range of the strong force is very limited. It acts over only very small distances, often smaller than the width of the atomic nucleus. The electromagnetic force, on the other hand, has an infinite range (though it becomes weaker with distance). Thus, two protons that are not close together will repel one another with the electromagnetic force, but two protons that are *very* close together will attract one another with the strong force.

There is yet another force acting within the nucleus of the atom. It is much weaker than even the electromagnetic force and is known, logically enough, as the *weak force.* (It is considerably stronger than the gravitational force, however.) The weak force is neither an attractive force, like the other three forces, nor a repulsive force, like electromagnetism. But, just like the other forces, it is responsible for certain interactions between subatomic particles. Specifically, the weak force sometimes changes one particle into another particle.

How's that again? Admittedly, the action of the weak force is difficult to understand, but the results it produces are quite striking. For instance, it is the weak force that is responsible, at least in part, for the fusion reactions that allow the sun to shine. Under certain circumstances, one subatomic particle can change into a different kind of subatomic particle, and it is the weak force that allows this to happen. When a particle changes into another particle, we say that it has *decayed.*

We'll have more to say about forces in a moment, but for now let's turn to another aspect of the subatomic world, the equivalence of matter and energy.

Amazing Fact Number 3
Matter is energy.

In classical physics—the physics of Isaac Newton and those who followed him in the eighteenth and nineteenth centuries—energy and matter were considered to be separate things. Energy is what allows matter to move. It comes in two different forms: *kinetic energy*, the energy of motion, and *potential energy*, the energy of position. When you pick a rock up off the ground, you use your own kinetic energy to give the rock potential energy. When you let go of the rock, as it moves toward the ground its potential energy is converted back into kinetic energy.

Sometimes heat and electricity are considered to be additional forms of energy, but these are actually types of kinetic energy, albeit on a very small scale. Heat is the motion of the molecules, atoms, and subatomic particles that make up matter. We detect this motion as a physical sensation because of special sensors in our skin that register the motion of molecules. Electricity is the motion of electrons in a common direction, usually flowing through substances that we call *electrical conductors*.

The division between matter and energy seems obvious, and yet Albert Einstein showed that it was only an illusion. Matter and energy, Einstein said, are simply different forms of the same thing, much as ice and water are different forms of the molecule H_2O. Just as ice can melt into water, so matter can sometimes turn into energy.

The atomic bomb is an example of Einstein's theory in action. An atomic explosion occurs when many atoms of uranium or plutonium break apart to form smaller atoms. In the process, a certain amount of the matter in the atoms is converted directly into energy, producing the explosion. This process is called *fission*, because it involves large

An atomic bomb explosion demonstrates Albert Einstein's theory that matter can turn into energy.

atoms "fissioning" (that is, breaking apart) to form smaller atoms. The force of the atomic bomb explosion is evidence of the huge amounts of energy bound up in relatively small amounts of matter.

Similarly, a hydrogen bomb heats the nuclei of hydrogen atoms to a very high temperature—that is, it makes them move at very high speeds—so that they collide with one another and knock one another apart, reforming into the larger nuclei of helium atoms. In the process, an even larger portion of matter is turned into energy, producing an even larger explosion. This process is called *fusion*, because it involves smaller atoms fusing together to form larger atoms.

Just as matter can turn into energy, so can energy turn into matter. Perhaps the best natural example of this is the cosmic-ray shower. A cosmic "ray" is actually a subatomic particle shooting through space at extremely high speeds, almost as fast as the speed of light. No one knows where such particles come from; perhaps they originate in supernovas or in the energetic matter surrounding black holes. When one of these particles enters the earth's atmosphere, it inevitably collides with particles in the air. The particle from space carries so much kinetic energy, however, that a certain amount of this energy is converted instantly into matter, in the form of a cascade of subatomic particles.

These are brand-new particles; they never existed before. They are formed out of pure energy, the kinetic energy of the cosmic-ray particle. Since each of these brand-new particles inherits a certain amount of kinetic energy from the cosmic-ray particle, it inevitably collides with still other particles in the atmosphere, and still more particles are created. The result is a shower of many particles created out of the energy of the particle from space.

In the 1930s, physicists began placing closed boxes full of photographic plates on mountaintops. The photographic plates, when developed, recorded the paths of cosmic-ray particles passing through them. This is how physicists discovered many of the types of subatomic particles not ordinarily found in atoms.

Nowadays, physicists can duplicate this particle-producing process in the laboratory, inside particle accelerators. Using giant electromagnets to accelerate particles to speeds close to that of light, they collide particles with one another and produce new particles out of pure energy. Hundreds of new subatomic particles have been discovered and studied in this manner.

Amazing Fact Number 4
Big particles are made up of smaller particles.

Just as the seemingly "indivisible" atom is actually made up of three kinds of smaller particles, so at least two of those smaller particles (and hundreds of particles not found in atoms) are made up in turn of even smaller particles. Protons and neutrons—the so-called nucleons—are made up of smaller particles called *quarks*. Just as the particles in atoms have both positive and negative electric charges, which cancel each other out to give the atom no overall charge, so the quarks have a special kind of charge known as *color charge*, which comes in three different varieties, often called red, green, and blue (after the primary colors of light).

This color charge has nothing to do with "real" color—i.e., the color of objects in the world around us—but the analogy is irresistible. Just as the three primary colors of light blend together to form a colorless white, so three quarks with different color charges join together inside a proton or neutron to form a colorless "white" nucleon. The quarks are held together inside the larger particle by a *color force*. This color force, oddly enough, becomes stronger with distance (up to a certain point, at least). For that reason, quarks are unable to escape from inside nucleons and are never seen by themselves. The color force, however, escapes the nucleon in the form of the strong force that holds nucleons together. Thus, the strong force is merely a vestige of the color force.

Neutrons and protons are not the only particles made up of quarks, though they are by far the most common. Collectively, all particles that are made of quarks are called *hadrons*. Electrons, on the other hand, are not made up of smaller particles and are known as *leptons*. There are five other known types of leptons: the *electron neutrino*, the *muon*, the *muon neutrino*, the *tau particle*, and the *tau neutrino*. (You don't need to memorize the names of these particles. Just be aware that they exist.)

Physicists now believe that the hadrons and leptons, along with certain particles that we can call "messenger particles" (which include *photons, gluons,* and *W particles*), are the fundamental particles out of which everything else is made. (We'll have more to say about messenger particles a little later.)

Amazing Fact Number 5
The subatomic world is "fuzzy."

Here in the world of the relatively large, we like to think that everything can be precisely measured. If we have two marbles sitting on the kitchen table, for instance, we know that there is a certain distance between them. Given a ruler and a sharp pair of eyes, we can measure that distance quite accurately; in theory, at least. In practice, of course, our measurement will be limited by the quality of our ruler and the sharpness of our eyes. But with better instruments—an improved ruler and a microscope, for instance—we could make a more accurate measurement. In theory, we could make our measurements as accurate as we want them to be.

In the 1920s, however, physicists realized that there was a theoretical limit to how accurate a measurement could be. No matter how good the instrument or how good our eyes, we could never measure the position of something more precisely than this theoretical limit.

More specifically, what physicists discovered was that if we wanted to make two different measurements of a subatomic particle—a measurement of its position, say, and a measurement of its motion—then both measurements could not be completely accurate. The more accurately we measure its position, for instance, the less accurately we can measure its motion, or vice versa. This is known formally as the *Heisenberg uncertainty principle,* or simply *quantum uncertainty.*

In the world of the relatively large, we are not bothered by quantum uncertainty because we do not need perfectly accurate measurements. Even precision manufacturing techniques are not perfectly accurate, but the small amounts of inaccuracy involved do not matter in practice. In the world of subatomic particles, on the other hand, these "small inaccuracies" might be so large that a million atoms could march abreast through a single measuring error. When we measure the position and movement of a subatomic particle, we must be a great deal more accurate than this.

But quantum uncertainty tells us that we can't be as accurate as we would like to be. This has nothing to do with our measuring instruments. It is a limitation of the universe itself. In a real sense, we can't measure both the position and movement of a particle at the same time because it can't *have* position and movement at the same time. As soon as we attempt to measure one, the other becomes "fuzzy." At least, this is one possible way of interpreting the uncertainty principle. German physicist Werner Heisenberg, the discoverer of the principle, interpreted it this way.

And, in fact, there is ample evidence that this quantum fuzziness is a genuine feature of the universe. In the core of our sun, for instance, the nuclei of hydrogen atoms are constantly smashing into one another, knocking one another apart so that they reform into the larger nuclei of helium atoms. This is the same hydrogen fusion process that takes place in hydrogen bombs, as we saw in Amazing Fact Number 3. This process is made possible by the tremendous heat at the core of the sun. (Heat is simply the motion of particles. Fast-moving particles are more likely to knock each other apart than slow-moving particles are.)

In the 1930s, when physicists first worked out the equations describing the hydrogen fusion processes inside the sun, they were startled to discover that it simply was not hot *enough* for self-sustaining hydrogen fusion to take place. According to the theory, the sun should not exist. Yet it does. How is this possible?

The problem has to do with protons. We saw a moment ago that protons repel one another with the electromagnetic force, but attract one another with the strong force. Since the electromagnetic force has a longer range than the strong force, two protons must be close together before the strong attraction takes over. Hydrogen fusion occurs when two hydrogen nuclei collide with one an-

other. Yet hydrogen nuclei contain protons—in fact, hydrogen nuclei *are* protons—and therefore will repel one another unless they are very close together. This is why hydrogen fusion takes place only at very high temperatures. The nuclei must be moving with enough kinetic energy to overcome the repulsive electromagnetic force until they are close enough for the strong attraction to overcome the repulsion. However, the core of the sun simply isn't hot enough most of the time for this to happen.

The reason that it happens anyway is quantum uncertainty. If it were possible for a physicist to enter the core of the sun and measure the distance between two protons, quantum uncertainty would prevent that physicist from being able to say definitively whether they were both close enough and had sufficient kinetic energy for fusion to take place. This uncertainty about the position of the particles actually allows the particles to "tunnel" through the electromagnetic forces pushing them apart and come close enough for the strong force to take over. Fusion takes place despite the fact that classical physics says that it should not.

As we said, the universe is fuzzy. It is not just a matter of our being unable to measure the posi-

Werner Heisenberg, a theoretical physicist, investigated atomic structure.

tion and motion of particles precisely; the particles themselves do not *have* a precise position and motion.

Well, we warned you that the subatomic world was a bit weird. But things are going to get weirder still. For instance . . .

Amazing Fact Number 6
Forces are particles.

Just as matter can be viewed as a form of energy (and vice versa), so can the forces that act between particles be viewed as particles themselves. We can describe the electromagnetic attraction between two particles, for instance, as being the result of a "messenger particle" that carries the force from one particle to the other. First, one particle "emits" the messenger particle, then the other particle "absorbs" it. In effect, the messenger particle says to the second particle, "You will be attracted to (or repelled by) the first particle," and the second particle acts accordingly. The second particle then sends a messenger particle to the first particle, ordering it to reciprocate the reaction.

The messenger particle that carries the electromagnetic force is called the *photon*, which happens to be the particle that light is made up of. This is no accident; light happens to be a form of *electromagnetic radiation*, produced by particles with an electric charge. Radio waves, which are also a form of electromagnetic radiation, are also made up of photons, as are gamma rays, X rays, and microwaves. The cosmic microwave background radiation, discovered by Penzias and Wilson (see Chapter One), can be looked at as a vast cloud of photons.

But where do the photons that carry the electromagnetic force come from? It is one of the primary laws of physics that energy cannot be created or destroyed—and matter is just a form of energy. When a particle such as an electron or a proton emits a messenger particle such as a photon, isn't the messenger particle created out of nothing? Doesn't this violate the rule that energy (or matter) cannot be created or destroyed?

The answer, in effect, is that it violates the letter of the law but not the spirit. Physicists only know that energy cannot be created or destroyed because they've never *seen* it happen. If it happened but physicists could never *see* it happen, then it would not really violate the law. And quantum uncertainty provides for such a circumstance.

Just as the uncertainty principle says that we cannot measure both a particle's position and motion at the same time with complete accuracy, it also says that we cannot measure both a particle's energy (and therefore its mass) and the amount of time that it has that energy at the same time with complete accuracy. Oddly, this means that if a particle of a certain mass exists for less than a certain amount of time, we will never know that it existed at all. The less energy (or mass) that the particle has, the longer it can exist without our being aware of it. A photon, with no mass at all, can potentially escape detection forever.

Thus, quantum uncertainty allows a particle to be created out of nothing as long as it vanishes back into nothing before it can be detected. Such particles that appear out of nothing and vanish into nothing are called *virtual particles*. The messenger particles that carry forces between other particles are one kind of virtual particle.

Interestingly, it is the mass of the messenger particle that determines the range of a force, that is, the distance over which the force can work. The range of the electromagnetic force is infinite because the photon has no mass. Therefore, a virtual photon can exist forever and carry its force over an infinite distance. The strong force, on the other hand, is carried by a messenger particle known as the *meson*. The meson is relatively massive, and therefore a virtual meson will exist for only a small amount of time. The messenger particle vanishes back into nothing before it can carry the force very far or be detected. This is why the strong force has a short range. The weak force, too, is carried by a relatively massive particle known as the W *particle* and thus has a short range. Gravity is carried by a particle called the *graviton*. Little is known about the graviton, but it must have no mass because the range of gravity is believed to be infinite.

Wait a minute! In the first chapter, we said that gravity is caused by the curving of space in the presence of matter. Now we are saying that it is carried by a particle called a graviton. Can't physicists make up their minds about these things?

The problem, as we said at the beginning of this chapter, is that it is impossible to describe the quantum world in ordinary language without resorting to metaphors. Both the curve in space and the graviton are metaphors for what really happens when objects attract one another gravitationally. They both describe the same thing, but they describe it in very different terms. In a sense, neither is a real description of what is happening; they are both approximate. Physicists use these descriptions to help organize their thoughts and to explain physics to nonphysicists; the real description of gravity and other forces is expressed in the mathematics that physicists use to calculate the interactions between particles.

When we describe gravity as a curve in space, we are said to be employing a *relativistic* description of gravity, because this description is taken from Einstein's theory of relativity. When we describe gravity as an exchange of messenger particles, we are said to be employing a *quantum* description of gravity, because it is based on the theory of quantum mechanics. Physicists would very much like to have a complete quantum description of gravity. Unfortunately, they have had a great deal of trouble producing such a description. As we shall see in the next chapter, such a description would greatly help physicists to understand what happened in the first, infinitesimally short, fraction of a second after the Big Bang.

Complete quantum description or not, we can still think of the gravitational force and other forces as being made of particles. In fact, we can think of the vacuum of space itself as being made up of particles. . . .

Amazing Fact Number 7
A vacuum isn't empty.

We are used to thinking of the vacuum of space as being utterly empty, except for the occasional particle of interstellar medium (see Chapter Two). And yet, just as Einstein viewed empty space as being every bit as real as matter, we can think of space as being made up of an infinite number of virtual particles, each existing too short a time to be detected by physicists. The "real" particles that make up the matter that surrounds us—the matter in this book, for instance, or the floor beneath your feet—are vastly outnumbered by this seething ocean of virtual particles that surrounds us every moment of the night and day. Physicists refer to this constant creation and destruction of virtual particles as *vacuum fluctuations.*

When particles are formed out of energy, as they are when a cosmic-ray particle collides with a particle in the earth's atmosphere, we can think of those new particles as being virtual particles that have received sufficient energy from the collision to become real particles. After receiving this energy, they are no longer in violation of the rule that says energy cannot be created or destroyed, and they may exist long periods of time, since it no longer matters whether or not they are detectable.

In fact, the only difference between the "real" particles in the matter that we see about us and the virtual particles of the vacuum is that the real particles have enough energy to allow them to exist long enough to be detected and the virtual particles do not. For this reason, physicists like to think of matter as an "excited vacuum."

It is an interesting fact of this creation of particles out of the vacuum that particles are always created in pairs. And that leads neatly to our next Amazing Fact. . . .

Amazing Fact Number 8
Every particle has an antiparticle.

Antimatter sounds like something out of science fiction. The Starship *Enterprise* of "Star Trek" fame is supposedly powered by antimatter engines. But antimatter itself is not fictional at all. It really exists, albeit in surprisingly small quantities.

When particles are created out of energy—or, to use a different metaphor, when virtual particles are given enough energy to become real particles—they are created in pairs, with one half of the pair being a "normal" particle and the other half being its antiparticle. When electrons are created, for instance, they are always created in tandem with antielectrons—or *positrons,* as they are better known. The positron is identical to the electron in every way, except that it has a positive electric charge. (The electron, you'll recall, has a negative electric charge.) It is this reversal of electric charges that makes the difference between a particle and its antiparticle. And in the same way, when protons are created, *antiprotons* are also created, and so forth.

At the time of creation, these particles generally go off in their separate ways. This is for the best, because when a particle encounters its antiparticle both are destroyed, being converted into pure energy and effectively reversing the process of their creation. This is called *particle–antiparticle annihilation,* and it explains why cosmic-ray showers don't result in an inevitable buildup of antimatter on earth; it doesn't take long for an antiparticle created in the shower to encounter its corresponding particle and convert back into energy.

Until recently, physicists were convinced that there was an inflexible rule of the universe that required matter and antimatter to be created in equal amounts. But this sets up a paradoxical situation that can be summed up in the question: Where is all the antimatter?

When the universe was created in the Big Bang, obviously a great deal of matter was created in the bargain, the matter that makes up the stars, planets, etc. But if an equal amount of antimatter was created, then why didn't all of these particles and antiparticles annihilate each other, leaving behind only photons? (A photon, strangely enough, is its own antiparticle, and doesn't undergo matter–antimatter annihilation.) Clearly, this didn't happen, so where is the antimatter that was presumably created in the Big Bang to balance out the normal matter that we see around us?

One possible answer is that the matter and antimatter created in the Big Bang somehow became separated, and now exist in different parts of the universe, where they cannot come into contact. But even if this is so—and scientists don't know of any way that this could happen—there should be a zone in space where the matter and antimatter regions touch. The interstellar medium of the matter region would come into contact with the interstellar medium of the antimatter region, and the two would gradually annihilate one another, producing vast bursts of gamma radiation. And yet such bursts of radiation have never been detected.

SOMETIMES IT SEEMS as though physicists, in exploring the ultimate nature of our universe, are trying to make things more complicated than they really need to be. The Amazing Facts in this chapter barely scratch the surface of quantum weirdness. If you'd like to learn more about the strange world of subatomic particles, you might want to look at some of the books mentioned in the bibliography at the end of this book, or just check out the physics section at your public or school library.

As complicated as all this may sound, though, physicists are trying to simplify our view of the universe; to show how the varied phenomena of the world around us, and of the subatomic universe that we cannot see with our eyes, are actually the result of a relatively simple set of underlying rules. In the next chapter, we'll see how this search for the underlying simplicity of nature has thrown surprising light on the nature of reality—and on the nature of our universe at the time of its creation.

FOUR

SYMMETRY

It has been suggested (and hinted at in the opening chapter of this book) that most human minds would have great difficulty grasping the size of the universe. It is too big; there is too much in it. Alas, we have only our relatively puny brains with which to assimilate this knowledge. Filling our brains with an understanding of something as large as the universe would be like pouring a thousand gallons of water into a quart bottle—it wouldn't fit.

Is this so? Are most humans really incapable of understanding the universe around them? If they are, then the quest to understand the Big Bang and the universe that emerged from it is futile from the very start. Why should scientists even bother?

Scientists bother because they know that the human brain isn't like a quart bottle. You don't have to fill it with all possible information about a subject in order for it to understand that subject. Rather, you only have to pour in a few relatively simple concepts and principles—the fewer, the better.

For instance, if you said that you understood automobile engines, would you mean that you were familiar with every nut and bolt and spark plug in every automobile engine ever built? Not very likely. It is possible to understand something without knowing every possible example of that something. In fact, it is possible to understand the *concept* of an automobile engine without even knowing what nuts and bolts are (though it is unlikely that you could become an auto mechanic on the basis of such knowledge).

Rather, when you say that you understand automobile engines, you mean that you have an abstract picture in your mind of an ideal automobile engine, a *conceptual* automobile engine, which has features in common with most real automobile engines. If you opened up the hood of a car and looked at an automobile engine that you'd never seen before, you'd probably be able to figure out in short order how it worked, even if it was designed somewhat differently from other automobile engines that you'd seen. Simply put, you would compare it with the ideal automobile engine in your mind and determine the ways in which it resembled that ideal engine and the ways in which it differed from it.

In the same way, when cosmologists seek to understand the universe and its origin, they are not seeking to learn the history of every star in the sky, or of every galaxy. That is a job best left to workaday astronomers, a job that will probably never be finished. Rather, they are attempting to understand the general concept of a "star" or a "galaxy," to find features that all stars and galaxies have in common, and to understand how these features fit into the universe as a whole and how they arose after the Big Bang. Most importantly, they are seeking to find the general rules and principles that make the universe the way it is. Some physicists believe that they are now very close to doing just that.

The search for the relatively simple underlying rules that give rise to the complex phenomena of the universe is called *reductionism*, because it is an attempt to reduce complexity to simplicity. Although it may sometimes seem as though scientists are making our world more complicated—and, indeed, this is sometimes the case—the true goal of science is to make things simpler. Ultimately, cosmologists hope to discover that the universe is a simple place indeed, that everything in the universe can be explained by two or three underlying principles or perhaps even one underlying principle.

The history of physics is full of examples of reductionism. Newton, for instance, reduced our understanding of orbiting planets and falling apples to a relatively simple understanding of the law of gravity. Dalton reduced the thousands of known chemical compounds to less than a hundred atomic elements. Quantum theory reduced Dalton's elements to an understanding of three subatomic particles. Quark theory reduced our understanding of hundreds of subatomic particles (most of which are not found in Dalton's atoms) to an understanding of a handful of quarks.

Most physicists now believe that our understanding of matter and forces, the twin concepts that are responsible in one way or another for everything we see in the universe around us, is about to become simpler still. It is possible that the dozens of quarks, leptons, and messenger particles are actually a single type of particle that we only perceive as being different particles. And the four forces that hold matter together may actually be a single superforce. To understand the universe and its origin, we need only to understand this single particle and this single force. In an odd sort of way, the universe may be simpler than an automobile engine.

The most powerful tool that physicists utilize in their search for the underlying simplicity of the universe is called *symmetry*. Appropriately, symmetry is a very simple tool. But, ironically, that very simplicity makes it a bit hard to understand. Perhaps we are so used to looking for complexity in our explanations of the universe that we have trouble recognizing simplicity when we see it.

Simply put, the concept of symmetry says that things can change without changing. In fact, it is possible that all the changes that we see taking place in the universe around us, from the movement of the planets in their orbits to the expansion of the universe itself, are taking place as a result of things *not* changing. Although we may see something as "changing," another change inevitably takes place somewhere in the universe that cancels it out, so that no overall change takes place.

As we said, symmetry is a simple concept that can be hard to understand. Let's look at it in more detail.

When most scientists say that something has symmetry, they mean that it can change in a way that produces no overall change. When an ordinary person talks about symmetry, on the other hand, he or she may be referring specifically to the shape of something but means pretty much the same thing. When we say that the shape of something is symmetrical, we mean that there are ways in which we can change that shape without actually changing it.

For example, we say that the shape of a butterfly is symmetrical because we can turn the butterfly around (or look at it in a mirror) without its shape actually changing. In fact, almost all living creatures have this kind of *mirror* (or *reflection*) *symmetry*. When you look at yourself in the mirror, your shape remains the same, though your mirror image is left-handed while you are right-handed (or vice versa). In terms of shape, human beings are symmetrical. In terms of handedness—right-handedness or left-handedness—we are not.

Similarly, we say that a rectangular object (such as this book) is symmetrical, because we can turn it upside down without changing its shape. We say that the book has *rotational symmetry*—or, more specifically, 180-degree rotational symmetry—because we can rotate it 180 degrees without its shape changing. On the other hand, if we rotate it only 90 degrees, its shape does change.

Of course, if you rotate your head—and therefore your point of view—along with the book, its shape will not change. We can say that the rotation of your head compensates for the rotation of the book, so that there is no overall change. Taken together, the two rotations cancel one another out.

A square object is even more symmetrical than a rectangular object, because you *can* rotate a square 90 degrees without its shape changing. And a circle is even more symmetrical than a square, because you can rotate a circle *any* number of degrees without its shape changing.

What does all of this have to do with the universe, or with physics? Well, there is little question that the universe is symmetrical. You can look at the universe from any position—lying on your side or standing on your head—and it looks the same. Of course, your local part of the universe may change—buildings may appear to be upside-down and people may seem to walk past with their feet above their heads—but the universe as a whole doesn't seem to change at all. Astronomers in Australia see much the same universe as do astronomers in the United States, though their viewpoints are upside-down relative to one another. Australian astronomers may see different stars and galaxies than American astronomers, but what they see still fits neatly within the general concept of stars and galaxies that originated with astronomers in the Northern Hemisphere. Further, physicists in Australia deduce the same laws of nature from their experiments as do physicists in the United States, despite the fact that they have been rotated 180 degrees relative to one another. The laws of the universe are not different for physicists who are "upside-down."

This may sound like a trivial observation, but it really isn't. In recent centuries, physicists have become fond of explaining the universe in terms of *conservation laws*. These "laws" have nothing to do with recycling paper or saving fuel or picking up litter; rather, they concern certain things that are *conserved*—left unchanged—despite the changes going on in the universe around them.

For instance, in the last chapter we said that energy (and therefore matter) cannot be created or destroyed. This is known formally as the *law of the conservation of energy*. It says, in effect, that energy is conserved—left unchanged—in the universe as a whole under all known circumstances. Stars and galaxies, not to mention human empires, may rise and fall, but there will always be (and has always been) exactly as much energy in the universe as there is today. The total energy of the universe cannot change.

A similar conservation law is called the *law of the conservation of angular momentum*. Roughly put, when we see an object spinning, whether that object is a top or a galaxy or an electron, it has angular momentum. The conservation law says that this angular momentum cannot be created or destroyed. It's only fair to ask, then, where angular momentum comes from when we see it.

A good example would be the spin that a professional baseball pitcher puts on a baseball. It would appear that this spin is created out of nothing when the pitcher throws the ball, and in a sense this is true. And yet the law of the conservation of angular momentum says that this cannot happen. We resolve this apparent contradiction through a loophole in this particular conservation law: angular momentum in one direction—clockwise, say—can cancel out angular momentum in the opposite direction—counterclockwise, in this case—just as a rotation of your head can cancel out a change in the shape of this book when you rotate it 90 degrees. If equal amounts of clockwise and counterclockwise rotation are created simultaneously, then the total angular momentum of the universe remains the same.

When the pitcher sends the ball spinning, say, clockwise, he sends his entire body spinning counterclockwise. The angular momentum of the ball in one direction and the angular momentum of the pitcher in the opposite direction precisely can-

The angular momentum the pitcher imparts to the ball is canceled out by the angular momentum of his body.

cel one another out. The pitcher does not spin as rapidly as the ball because his body has a much greater radius (the distance from its center to its edges) than the ball, and the angular momentum is spread out over this entire radius. When his foot then presses against the ground, the angular momentum is in turn absorbed by the entire planet, which has such a huge radius that this fresh supply of angular momentum does not produce any noticeable change in rotation. Thus, while it may be true that the angular momentum that the pitcher imparts to the ball is created out of nothing, it is compensated for by the angular momentum of his body. The angular momentum of the universe as a whole is unchanged. No conservation law is violated.

The fact that the angular momentum of the universe is conserved has some surprising applications. For instance, if you've ever seen a figure-skating exhibition, you know that the skater will often finish his or her program by spinning rapidly on one skate. The skater gains this angular momentum by kicking the ice with one skate, thus imparting an equal amount of angular momentum in the opposite direction to the planet, which absorbs it totally. But then a surprising thing happens. The skater actually begins rotating faster and faster. Where does *this* angular momentum come from?

The answer is that the skater's sudden increase in rotation speed is a result of the fact that his or her angular momentum did *not* increase.

When the skater first begins spinning, his or her arms are outstretched. But then the skater pulls the arms closer to the body, or holds them up straight above the head, thus reducing the skater's radius considerably. As the radius shrinks, the skater's angular momentum is spread over a smaller and smaller area. And just as the pitcher's greater radius causes him to spin more slowly than the ball he pitched, so the skater's reduced radius causes him or her to spin faster and faster. If this did not happen, then the skater's overall angular momentum would be reduced, and this is, literally, against the law. Thus, the skater speeds up. It is not unreasonable to suggest that the universe speeds up the skater so that its overall angular momentum will not change. The change in the skater's speed is a result of the universe's refusal to change.

The really remarkable thing about all of this is that the law of conservation of angular momentum is a direct result of the fact that the universe is symmetrical. It can be shown logically (though we will not do it in this book) that if angular momentum were *not* conserved, then an astronomer in Australia would see the universe differently than an astronomer on the opposite side of the world, because he or she is looking at it from a different orientation. Similarly, a physicist in Australia would deduce a different set of physical laws governing the universe than a physicist in the United States. Since we know that this does not happen, we know that angular momentum must be conserved. In fact, if physicists had not discovered the law of the conservation of angular momentum through experimentation, they might have been able to deduce it from the symmetry of the universe.

In the 1930s, the German physicist Emmy Nother demonstrated that all of the conservation laws of physics—and there are quite a few—are a result of symmetries in the universe. Today, physicists believe that everything in the universe, from particles to stars to galaxies to the Big Bang itself, can be explained in terms of conservation laws. Thus, everything in the universe is a result of symmetry.

As we saw earlier in this chapter, physicists use the term symmetry rather broadly, to mean anything that can "change" without changing. The fact that a physicist in a moving vehicle—an airplane, say, or a rocket ship—would deduce the same physical laws as a physicist standing still on the surface of the earth, for instance, is considered a kind of symmetry. The universe, then, is not only symmetrical in terms of orientation in space—i.e., whether you look at it from Australia or the United States—but in terms of movement through space. Perhaps surprisingly, this is why the law of the conservation of energy exists. If energy were not conserved, then the laws of the universe would look different to a moving physicist than to a stationary physicist. (Even more surprisingly, Albert Einstein used this fact as the basis of his Special Theory of Relativity, where he showed that time would be perceived differently by an observer, say, in a spaceship than by an observer on the surface of a planet that was motionless relative to the spaceship. If time did *not* change as a result of motion, then a physicist in the spaceship would deduce different physical laws than a physicist on the surface of the planet, and this would violate the symmetry of the universe. Thus, time actually changes as a result of relative motion.)

Because symmetry is so important to physicists, an entire branch of mathematics has been developed to describe various forms of symmetry. This branch of mathematics is called *group theory*. Using the equations of group theory, physicists have discovered many subtle and unexpected symmetries in the universe around us, many of which are virtually impossible to describe (alas!) in nonmathematical terms.

It has been shown, for instance, that all of the forces in the universe—gravity, electromagnetism, and the weak and strong forces—are the result of symmetries in the universe. In effect, these forces exist to compensate for changes in the universe in such a way that no overall change will take place. Just as our ice skater is speeded up by the refusal of the universe to change its angular momentum, so the forces of gravity, and so on, are a way of enforcing the essential changelessness of the universe. It's not necessary for you to understand precisely why this is the case. Just realize that it is symmetry that makes the universe the way it is. (If you would like to know more about it, however, the bibliography at the end of this book lists a number of good books on the subject.)

ALTHOUGH PHYSICISTS have found many symmetries in the universe, they would much prefer that there were fewer of them. In fact, if it turned out that everything in the universe could be explained by a single symmetry, physicists would be extremely happy. They would have reduced the universe to its ultimate simplicity, showing that everything in the universe is the way it is because the universe needs to be symmetrical, that is, essentially unchanging.

It's hard to imagine, though, that something as complex as our universe could be explained by a single symmetry. After all, there are still dozens of particles and four forces to explain. But what if we could reduce the four forces to one force and the dozens of particles to a single particle?

The scientific theories that attempt to show that two or more forces of nature are actually different aspects of a single superforce are called *unified field theories*. The search for a verifiable unified field theory has gone on for much of this century. In fact, it began when only two forces—gravity and electromagnetism—were known. The driving force, as it were, behind these early unified field theories was Albert Einstein, arguably the greatest physicist (and perhaps the greatest scientist) of this century.

And yet even the great Einstein could not succeed in showing that the known forces were actually manifestations of a single superforce. Probably the reason for this was that Einstein was born before his time. The forces of nature were not yet fully understood. All of the forces were not yet known. And one of the forces that Einstein chose to unify, gravity, has proved to be the hardest of all forces to explain with a unified field theory.

In the 1960s, however, physicists succeeded in showing that another pair of forces, electromagnetism and the weak force, are actually the result of a single underlying force, that we now call the *electroweak force*. This amazing discovery was made possible by the realization that the electromagnetic and weak forces behaved differently at different temperatures.

Earlier, we said that heat is actually just the kinetic energy—the energy of motion—of atoms, molecules, and subatomic particles. Temperature, then, is just the average kinetic energy of all particles in a given area of space. When we say that the temperature in a house is very high, we mean that the average kinetic energy of the air molecules in the house is high. Put another way, the air molecules are moving very quickly. When we say that the temperature of the house is low, we mean that the air molecules are moving relatively slowly.

In the same way, when we speak of the temperature of subatomic particles, we are talking about their kinetic energy. When a particle moves very quickly, we say it is hot. When a particle moves slowly, we say it is cold. If the average speed of a group of particles is high, we say that the temperature of the particles is high. If the average speed of a group of particles is low, we say that the temperature of the particles is low.

The temperature (speed) of a particle will affect the way in which it interacts with other particles. We can make an analogy here with a baseball game. The batter at the plate may find it harder to hit a fastball than a slowball, because it rushes too quickly past the bat; while the catcher may find it easier to catch the fastball than the slowball, because it speeds straight into the catcher's mitt instead of falling into the dirt. The interactions between these players and the ball is affected by the speed of the ball, but in different ways. We might say that the interaction between the batter and the ball grows weaker with higher speeds, while the interaction between the catcher and the ball grows stronger.

Similarly, the interactions between particles are affected by the kinetic energy of the particles. The electromagnetic and weak forces both grow stronger as the particles affected by these forces gain more energy, but the weak force grows stronger faster with increasing temperature than the electromagnetic force does. However, at a certain very high temperature, the two forces have an identical strength. They become symmetric. Changing from the weak to the electromagnetic at this temperature is no change at all; thus, we can regard them as a single electroweak force.

Originally, this theory was worked out in terms of the symmetries involved, using the equations of group theory to show how the forces would change and become symmetric at a high temperature. However, it was subsequently verified by testing interactions between fast-moving (and therefore hot) particles in a particle accelerator. The theory held up beautifully. The electromagnetic and weak forces were shown conclusively to be two aspects of the same force.

Inspired by the success of this electroweak theory, physicists in the 1970s began work on even more ambitious unified theories, ones that would unify the strong force with the electroweak force. Such theories, which would unify all of the known forces except gravity, are called *grand unification theories* (or *GUTs*) by physicists. So far, physicists have been less successful with GUTs than with the electroweak theory, but substantial progress has been made. It turns out that the strong force, like the batter in our metaphorical baseball game, becomes weaker at higher temperatures, and in fact there is a very high temperature at which it becomes identical to the electroweak force. This temperature is so incredibly high, however, that no particle accelerator on earth can make particles move fast enough to verify the theory. Physicists do not like to accept a theory unreservedly until they have solid experimental proof that it is valid. Thus, GUTs must be taken with a certain grain of salt, however good they may look on paper.

Fortunately, there is a way in which GUTs may be proven outside of particle accelerators and without generating extremely high temperatures.

Grand unification theories all make the rather astonishing prediction that protons, some of the most important constituents of matter, will eventually fall apart into smaller particles. Though physicists have long believed that protons were completely stable—that a proton would effectively be around forever—GUTs say that, on the average, a proton will fall apart after roughly a million billion billion billion years. That's a long time, and it might seem futile for physicists to observe a proton that long to see if it falls apart.

There is, however, an easier way. This figure for the life of a proton is merely an average. Many protons will die much sooner. Therefore, physicists can gather a million billion billion billion protons together, usually in the form of a large vat of water, and wait for *one* proton to decay in the course of a year. Several proton-decay detectors have now been constructed and placed deep beneath the earth in abandoned mines, where they will be protected from cosmic-ray showers that might mimic the behavior of a decaying proton. So far, no proton decays have been detected, but physicists are still hopeful that GUTs will be vindicated.

This has not stopped physicists from going beyond GUTs to an ultimate unified field theory, one that unites all four forces: electromagnetism, the weak force, the strong force, and the hardest of all forces to unify with the rest, gravity. The problem, as we saw in the last chapter, is that no one

An underground proton-decay detector is basically a tank of water with devices sticking into it to detect decaying.

has yet developed a successful quantum description of gravity to replace Einstein's relativistic description, though many physicists are now attempting to do so. One theory developed in this attempt is known as *supersymmetry* (*SUSY* for short). This theory remains highly speculative at present, however.

An even more exciting attempt to unify all of the four forces was launched in 1984 with the new *superstring theory*, which grew out of an earlier theory proposed in the late 1960s. Superstring theory reduces the universe to what may be the ultimate state of symmetry. According to this theory, *all* of the known fundamental particles, including all quarks and leptons, are actually identical. In effect, they are all the same type of particle.

How can this be? In the past, the fundamental particles have been viewed by physicists as tiny points in space. Like a point in geometry, they were thought to have no size or dimensions at all but to be infinitely small. What made them distinct particles was that each had its specific identifying properties, such as mass, charge, spin, and so forth.

Superstring theory, on the other hand, views each particle as having a single dimension: length. In effect, all fundamental particles are tiny "strings." Further, these strings vibrate, rather like plucked guitar strings. The only differences between the various fundamental particles are in the way they are vibrating. (To continue the guitar string metaphor, we could say that each particle is playing a different "note.") These vibrations show themselves to physicists as the identifying properties of the particle, such as charge and spin.

Superstring theory also unifies all of the forces of nature, including gravity, into a single superforce. The way in which it does this is highly mathematical, and we will not go into it here, but scientists who work with superstring theory believe that it may be the theory that finally reduces the universe to the simplest possible state. This theory is not yet fully worked out, however.

Unfortunately, no one has yet devised a way to verify superstring theory experimentally, and no one is even sure that it can either be verified or disproved in the near future. For that reason, some physicists are reluctant to accept superstring theory at all; others are accepting it only tentatively. Experimental verification notwithstanding, however, superstring theory may be the most exciting and important idea to emerge from physics since quantum mechanics itself.

Perhaps the most remarkable thing about both supersymmetry and superstrings, the two major theories that attempt to unify gravity with the other three forces, is that both assume we live in an eleven-dimensional universe. We are all familiar, of course, with the three traditional dimensions of length, breadth, and depth. They are the three directions—dimensions—in which we are free to move, and thus we say that we live in a three-dimensional world. Einstein showed that time was also a dimension, though not in the same way that the other three are, since we are only free to move in one direction through time, and we are not free to stand still in it. According to Einstein, we live in a four-dimensional universe, with three dimensions of space and one dimension of time.

According to supersymmetry and superstring theory, on the other hand, there are *ten* dimensions of space in addition to the one dimension of time. We are not aware of the seven additional dimensions of space, because we are not free to move through them. And the reason that we are not free to move through these seven dimensions is that they are extremely small, much smaller than the size of a quark, while the other three space dimensions are large—and still expanding.

Where are these additional dimensions? They are all around us, at every point in space. This is, of course, nearly impossible to visualize, though it's rather fun to make the attempt. Don't feel bad if you fail, though. In Chapter Six, we'll discuss the possible reasons why these extra dimensions are so much smaller than the three space dimensions with which we are familiar.

WHAT DOES this discussion of symmetry have to do with the origin of the universe? We said a few moments ago that the forces of nature become unified—that is, effectively identical—at extremely high temperatures. However, such temperatures almost never occur in the universe today, not even in the hearts of stars. For this reason, physicists say that the symmetry between the forces of nature is *broken* or *hidden*. When we look at the universe today, we see four different forces rather than a single superforce.

But there was a time when the entire universe was at such incredibly high temperatures that all of the forces were unified, and there was only a single superforce. This was during the fraction of a second immediately after the Big Bang. Thus, at the moment the universe was created, it existed in a state of ultimate simplicity and symmetry, with all forces and particles identical. As the universe cooled off, however, the individual forces "froze out" of the single superforce that existed in the very beginning, in much the same way that ice "freezes out" of water as the temperature of the water drops. The symmetry was broken.

Physicists on earth have no way of re-creating the temperatures that were present at the time of the Big Bang in order to verify their grand unification theories. But by studying the origin of the universe, they can effectively treat the Big Bang itself as if it were the greatest high-energy physics laboratory of them all, a particle accelerator that encompassed the entire universe.

And, in turn, the theories that physicists develop about the unification of forces at high temperatures can cast light on how our universe came to be. We may someday even be able to answer the ultimate question: Why does the universe exist? Why is there something rather than nothing?

At this point, you have all the background information you need to understand what the universe was like immediately after the Big Bang. In the next chapter, then, we will begin looking at the birth of the universe itself.

BEGINNINGS

We can roughly divide the origin of the universe into three parts: the part that cosmologists are very sure of, the part that they are moderately sure of, and the part that they aren't sure of at all. In this chapter, we'll talk about the first two, the parts about which cosmologists have at least a modicum of confidence. In the next chapter, we'll talk about the part of the origin of the universe that still remains highly speculative. In some ways, this is the most fascinating part of all.

One of the things that cosmologists are not yet sure about is the Big Bang itself. It is not yet possible to give a definitive answer to the questions: What was the Big Bang and why did it happen? However, as we shall see in the next chapter, there has been a great deal of speculation recently on this subject, and it may not be long before a definitive (or almost definitive) answer is at hand. For the moment, however, we will simply take the Big

Bang as a given—a huge explosion in which time and space began expanding.

It is important, by the way, to realize that space itself originated in the Big Bang. It is tempting to think of the universe before the Big Bang as being a vast, possibly infinite, expanse of empty space, much like the space between the galactic clusters today. The Big Bang, then, would have flung matter into this nothingness. But this is not what happened. Space itself was created in the Big Bang. Remember that Einstein and all subsequent cosmologists have viewed space as being every bit as real as matter. (And, in fact, physicists now view empty space as a sea of virtual particles, as we saw in Chapter Three.) Thus, space is now expanding along with the galaxies and stars that exist within it and has been expanding ever since the Big Bang.

Surprisingly, cosmologists actually have a clearer picture of what the universe was like during the period immediately after the Big Bang—the part that they are *very* sure of—than they have of what the universe is like today. The reason is that the contents of the universe were a great deal simpler then. The universe was filled with a hot soup of particles that behaved like a hot gas trapped in a box—which, in fact, it was, if the universe can be regarded as a giant box. The photons in the cosmic microwave background radiation discovered by Penzias and Wilson are the last remnant of that hot soup, still trapped inside the box of the universe. Everything else has evolved into more complex forms, such as planets, stars, and galaxies. By analyzing the cosmic background radiation, cosmologists have been able to learn important things about the hot soup of particles that filled the universe 18 billion years ago.

Perhaps the single most important thing that we know about conditions immediately after the Big Bang is that the universe was extremely dense. That is, all of the matter (and, therefore, energy) in it was compressed together very tightly. On the other hand, we do not know how *big* the universe was immediately after the Big Bang, because—as we saw in Chapter Two—we do not know how big the universe is now. If the universe is infinitely large today, then it would have been infinitely large then, because there is no way that the universe could go from having a finite size to having an infinite one. On the other hand, if the universe has a finite size today, then it had a finite (and relatively small) size then.

On the other hand, we do know how large the *visible* universe would have been immediately after the Big Bang. The visible universe is that portion of the universe that an observer, imaginary or otherwise, would under ideal viewing conditions be able to see. In Chapter Two, we pointed out that the visible universe today has a radius of about 18 billion light-years, because that is how far light has been able to travel in the approximately 18 billion years since the Big Bang. Anything outside of that 18-billion-light-year radius would be invisible to us because the light from it has not reached us yet.

This would be true for observers anywhere in the universe, not just on earth. Observers more than 18 billion light-years from earth would not be able to see us either, no matter how good their telescopes were.

In the period immediately after the Big Bang, the visible universe was much smaller. One minute after the Big Bang, for instance, the visible universe would have had a radius of one light-minute, that is, the distance that light can travel in one minute. The actual size of the universe, however, would probably have been larger, perhaps infinitely larger.

Surprisingly, it is possible for the actual size of the universe to increase faster than the size of the visible universe. This is surprising because it means that the universe might be expanding faster than the speed of light. Einstein's Special Theory of Relativity states quite firmly that nothing can move faster than the speed of light. Einstein, however, was talking about the motion of matter and radiation through space. The expansion of the universe is not movement through space, but the expansion of space itself. And Einstein's theory does not forbid space from expanding faster than the speed of light.

Things happened very quickly right after the Big Bang. Compared to the speed of events in the seconds and minutes after the creation of the universe, the modern universe moves at something a great deal slower than a snail's pace. Thus, it is common for physicists to divide the seconds, and even fractions of seconds, after the Big Bang into *eras*. Although it may seem odd to speak of an interval of time shorter than a second as an era, it makes sense in terms of the rapid pace of events. And, as we will see in Chapter Seven, there may be other reasons as well for thinking of the seconds after the Big Bang as being equivalent to vast periods of time in the universe today.

The times involved in discussing these eras are so short that we must adopt a special numbering system, called *exponential notation*, for describing the fractions of a second involved. Otherwise, the pages of this book would be filled with zeros, or the words billionths and billionths repeated over and over again. In exponential notation, we might speak of a time 10^{-35} seconds after the Big Bang. This refers to a fraction of a second that would be written in decimal as 1 preceded by thirty-four (thirty-five minus one) zeros and a decimal point, like this:

.00000000000000000000000000000000001

In the same way, 10^{-12} seconds would be written as a 1 preceded by eleven zeros and a decimal point. And so forth.

The earliest era of which physicists can speak with any confidence at all is the so-called *grand unification era*, or *GUT era*, the era during which the strong, electromagnetic, and weak forces were still united in a single superforce. (Gravity, however, had already frozen out as a separate force by this time.) This era began at 10^{-43} (that is, 1 preceded by forty-two zeros and a decimal point) seconds after the Big Bang and ended at 10^{-35} seconds after the Big Bang. When we say that physicists are confident about this era, we don't mean that they know exactly what was taking place during it. The grand unification theories—GUTs—that describe this era are still being worked out and have not been verified experimentally. They may undergo considerable modification before they are accepted by all physicists and cosmologists around the world. Nonetheless, most cosmologists are reasonably certain that there actually was a time when the strong, electromagnetic, and weak forces were unified and that it took place roughly during this period after the Big Bang.

There were only two kinds of particles during the GUT era, which we might describe as matter particles and messenger particles. The former included all of the leptons and quarks that we discussed in Chapter Three, and the latter included all of the particles that carry forces between particles, including photons and gluons. Because of the conditions that existed during the GUT era, all matter particles were effectively identical, as were all messenger particles. Thus, we can say that only two types of particles existed, as opposed to the dozens that exist today. And only two forces existed, gravity and the grand unified force. (And, because the grand unified force was so much stronger than gravity, it was the only force that really mattered in terms of interactions between these rapidly moving particles.) All of these particles existed in a dense, hot soup.

The universe was quite simple during the GUT era, and extremely hot. The temperature of the universe during the GUT era was greater than 1,000,000,000,000,000—or one million billion—degrees Kelvin. This is known to physicists as the *grand unification temperature,* because it is the temperature at which the grand unification of forces takes place.

But as the universe expanded, it was also cooling off. Although the amount of energy in the universe remained the same—energy, as we have stated repeatedly, cannot be created or destroyed—it was being spread over a larger and larger area. Thus, the kinetic energy available in any given area of space was shrinking even as the universe grew, and therefore the temperature dropped.

As the universe cooled below one million billion degrees Kelvin, the strong force suddenly split apart from the electroweak force, and the symmetry between quarks and leptons disappeared. The universe was less symmetrical and more complex, because there were now three forces, two of them of considerable strength. This happened at 10^{-35} seconds after the Big Bang and is called the *GUT freezing,* that is, the point at which the strong force froze out from the grand unified force. The electromagnetic and weak forces, however, were still unified into a single electroweak force. This might be called the *electro-weak era*. Physicists are much more confident about the way things were in the electroweak era than they are about the way things were in the grand unification era, because we can actually duplicate the conditions of the electroweak era in particle accelerators.

As the temperature continued to drop, however, the electroweak force froze out into the electromagnetic and weak forces, and things became quite interesting, because the undifferentiated sea of quarks and leptons that had filled the universe until this time began to change into particles much more like those found in the universe today. At about 10^{-6} seconds after the Big Bang, the universe entered the *hadron era*.

Because temperatures were now lower, and the kinetic energy of particles smaller, the quarks in the cosmic soup were able to bind together to form the larger particles that we call hadrons—protons, neutrons, and so forth. This process is called *hadronization*. The hadron era may have been the last time that free quarks—quarks that are not part of larger particles—were seen in the universe, although some physicists believe that a few "fossil quarks" may have been left over from the hadron era and may still exist in the universe today. Attempts to detect these quarks in the laboratory have met with mixed success, however.

The tremendous energies present in the universe at this time—temperatures of just under one million billion degrees Kelvin—caused brand-new hadrons to be created in vast numbers out of the virtual particles of the vacuum, just as particles are created in cosmic-ray showers today but on a much larger scale. Since hadrons and antihadrons were created in equal numbers (or, as we shall see in a moment, in *roughly* equal numbers), these newly created particles annihilated into gamma rays as soon as they encountered their antiparticles, which was almost as soon as they came into existence. But the annihilated particles were instantly replaced by still more newly created particles, so that the number of hadrons in the universe remained more or less the same throughout the hadron era. The same was true of leptons and antileptons, which were also being created out of the virtual particles of the vacuum.

When the hadron era ended—an event that took place roughly 10^{-3} seconds after the Big Bang—a violent change came over the universe. The temperature in the universe ceased to be high enough to create hadrons out of the vacuum, so that new hadrons were no longer available to replace the ones lost to particle-antiparticle annihilation. A wholesale annihilation of hadrons took place. The number of hadrons in the universe plunged precipitously.

If equal amounts of hadrons and antihadrons had been created during the hadron era, the annihilation of the hadrons should have been total, a problem we discussed in Chapter Three. Every hadron in existence would have encountered its corresponding antiparticle, and all would have been annihilated. Shortly after the end of the hadron era, there should have been no hadrons left in the universe at all, a state that would remain true in the universe today. Since protons and neutrons, the most common of the hadrons, are a vital part of the matter that we see around us today, the universe as we know it could not exist if all hadrons had been annihilated. Why didn't this happen?

The answer to this is quite complex, and we won't go into it here in any detail. Suffice it to say that physicists have discovered a peculiar *asymmetry* (the opposite of a symmetry) in the universe concerning the way in which particles and antiparticles are created from the vacuum. Presumably this asymmetry is balanced out by a compensating asymmetry elsewhere in the universe, so that the overall symmetry of the universe is preserved, but at present this is only partially understood. As a result of this asymmetry, slightly more hadrons were created during the electroweak era than antihadrons—roughly one billion and one hadrons for every one billion antihadrons. At the end of the electroweak era, all of the antihadrons and all but one in a billion of the hadrons were annihilated. The remaining one in a billion hadrons make up the bulk of the matter that we see in the universe today. Solid matter in the modern universe is only the tiniest residue of the matter created in the Big Bang.

The era that followed the hadron era, after the hadron annihilation had taken place, is known as the *lepton era*. Just as hadrons were created out of the vacuum during the hadron era, so leptons, such as electrons and neutrinos, were created out of the vacuum during the lepton era (as they had been during the hadron era, though they were overshadowed then by the creation of hadrons). This was possible because leptons, having on the average less mass than hadrons, required less energy to create. The temperature at the beginning of the lepton era was roughly one trillion degrees Kelvin. The universe was still so dense that just the particles in an area of the universe one centimeter on all sides would have weighed a thousand tons. The visible universe was still less than one light-second in radius.

As the temperature of the universe fell below the level at which leptons could be created out of the vacuum, the leptons and antileptons began to annihilate just as the hadrons and antihadrons had annihilated at the end of the hadron era. And, just as there was a slight imbalance of hadrons to antihadrons at the end of the hadron era, so there was now a slight imbalance of leptons to antileptons, just enough to leave behind one out of every billion leptons created during the lepton era. Those are the leptons that, along with the hadrons left over from the hadron annihilation, make up the matter in the universe today.

Thus ended the lepton era. At this point, the matter in the universe had been reduced to one one-billionth what it had been a fraction of a second earlier, and the universe was dominated by the only major type of particle that had not undergone massive annihilation: the photon. As we noted in Chapter Three, the photon is its own antiparticle and does not undergo annihilation; hence, all of the photons created during the hadron and lepton eras remained in existence as the universe cooled and are, in fact, still in existence today, mostly in the form of the cosmic microwave background radiation detected by Penzias and Wilson. To this day, photons—the particles of electromagnetism—outnumber leptons and hadrons—the particles of matter—by a billion to one throughout the universe. The era following the lepton era is known, therefore, as the *photon era*. In fact, we might still be living in the photon era today, were it not that the photons gradually lost the energy that they possessed roughly one second after the Big Bang. At that time, most of the energy of the universe was in the photons; today, most of it is in matter, so that physicists say we now live in the *matter era*.

You might notice that no mention has been made so far of atoms in the early universe. The reason for this is that there were no atoms in the early universe. It was much too hot for electrons to remain in orbit around protons. In fact, for most of the period we have discussed so far, it was too hot for neutrons and protons to bind together to form a nucleus. Even if, for the tiniest instant, an atomlike configuration of particles had formed, it would have been broken apart by the fiercely energetic activity of the seethingly hot early universe. Of course, protons can be viewed as the nuclei of hydrogen atoms, since the nucleus of a hydrogen atom consists of a single proton. In that sense, then, hydrogen nuclei came into existence during the hadron era, but full-fledged hydrogen atoms did not form then and would not form for some time to come.

At a little less than four seconds after the Big Bang, things had cooled off enough for the nuclei of the next larger atom, helium, to form. Shortly after that, however, the universe became too cool for nucleosynthesis—the creation of atomic nuclei from protons and neutrons—to take place at all. At that point, the basic elements of the universe (or, more properly, their nuclei) had pretty much finished forming. Roughly 70 percent of the universe was now in the form of hydrogen nuclei and 30 percent in the form of helium nuclei, which are pretty much the proportions of these elements in the universe today. Even after these nuclei had formed, however, it was still much too hot for atoms to form around them. In fact, it remained too hot for atoms to form for the next 700,000 years!

You may be surprised to learn that during this entire period, that is, the first 700,000 years of the universe's existence, the entire universe was opaque. This means that light could not pass freely through it. The reason is that, because atoms had not yet formed, the universe was filled with free electrons. And electrons tend to absorb photons, the particles of light. A photon could not travel very far through this early universe without being absorbed by an electron. Of course, for every photon absorbed by an electron, another photon would have been released by an electron. Thus, the universe would have glowed brightly but would have been as dense as a superthick fog. Any observer in the middle of the early universe would have been unable to see a hand held in front of his or her face (assuming that hands could have existed in the absence of atoms, which isn't very likely).

Then, 700,000 years after the Big Bang, the universe cooled to the point where electrons, through the electromagnetic force, could become bound to nuclei and form atoms. To our imaginary observer, it would have been as though the fog had suddenly lifted. The universe would have become transparent. Normal matter had come into existence. In effect, the universe was a giant nebula of hydrogen and helium gases.

Because the atoms in the early universe were entirely those of hydrogen and helium, you might wonder where the heavier elements came from, such as the carbon and oxygen atoms that are so vital to living creatures. The answer is that many of them were formed much later, in the hearts of stars, where nucleosynthesis continues until this very day. But the majority of elements, which cannot be created even in stars, are created in supernova explosions, the only place in the modern universe where temperatures are available that are in any way comparable to those present shortly after the Big Bang.

From our description so far, it would seem as if the universe 700,000 years after the Big Bang was still an undifferentiated soup of hot particles, though by now the particles were atoms instead of quarks, leptons, and hadrons. How did we get from this smooth, soupy universe to the relatively bumpy universe full of stars, galaxies, and clusters of galaxies we see today?

That's a good question, and no one has yet come up with a completely satisfactory answer to it. Cosmologists would find the present universe much easier to explain if it were *still* an undifferentiated soup of particles, albeit a lot thinner and cooler than the soup of particles that existed 18 billion years ago. But if this were the case, there would be no cosmologists in existence to debate the question, so perhaps it is worth all of the difficulty that it may take to find the answer.

You might be tempted to think that stars formed first, from little whirlpools of hydrogen and helium in this primordial gas, then grouped together gravitationally into galaxies. But you would be wrong. The best present evidence is that galaxies actually formed before stars, as vast pools of gas in which stars then proceeded to form. But how did these pools of gas form?

One possibility is that they formed around cracks in space that came into existence almost immediately after the Big Bang. How can cracks

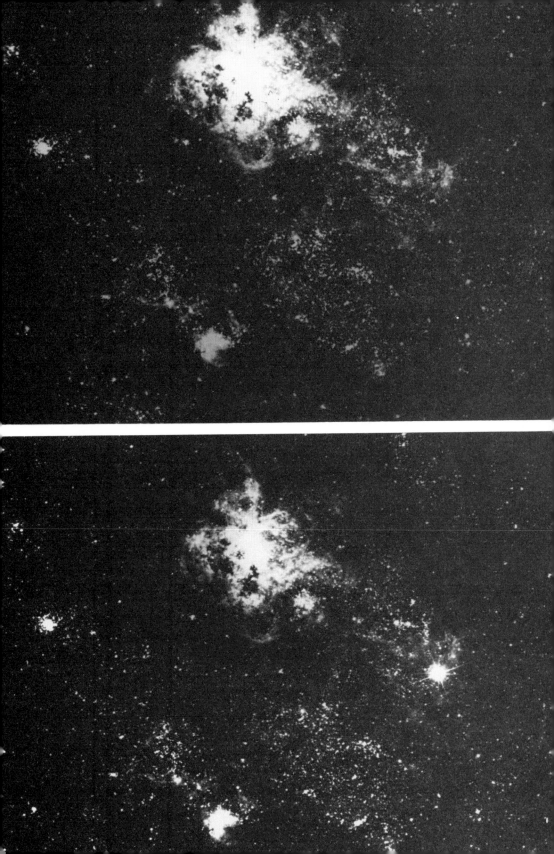

form in space? We saw earlier that the four forces of nature that are known today are believed to have "frozen out" of a single superforce during the fraction of a second immediately after the Big Bang. However, this freezing may not have taken place evenly over the entire universe at a single instant. Or more likely, it may have taken place at several isolated points in the universe—in several *domains*, as cosmologists phrase it—and then spread across the universe in the course of a fraction of a second. This is analogous to the way that the surface of a pond freezes in cold weather. And just as cracks form in the ice where two or more freezing domains come together, so cracks may have formed in the universe where two or more domains of freezing forces came together.

These cracks might manifest themselves as extremely large and dense objects called *cosmic strings* (not to be confused with the type of strings predicted by the superstring theory discussed in the last chapter). A cosmic string would be extremely long—perhaps stretching all the way across the universe—and microscopically thin. Yet, like a black hole, it would be so dense and

Before and after photographs of Supernova 1987A were taken eighteen years apart. The image at top is from 1969; the lower one, from 1987, shows the bright supernova at the right.

heavy that it would produce immense amounts of gravity, attracting matter toward it from all over the universe. The gaseous hydrogen and helium atoms in the early universe may have gathered around these cosmic strings, which is why astronomers now see the galaxies as forming into clusters that are almost stringlike in shape.

ONCE PROTOGALAXIES formed out of the hydrogen and helium gases of the early universe, and stars began to form as localized clusters of this gas collapsed under their own gravitational attraction, the universe was well on its way to becoming the one that we see around us today. The details of how the universe progressed from the cosmic soup left over after the Big Bang to the universe of stars and galaxies are still being filled in by cosmologists, physicists, and astronomers, but the above description should give you a rough idea of the process.

For the moment, however, we are going to shift to an even more fascinating aspect of cosmology, albeit one that remains extremely speculative: the Big Bang itself. And we may even catch a glimpse of what the universe was like *before* it was born!

SIX

SINGULARITY

As we push ever backward toward the Big Bang itself, into times even earlier than the beginning of the GUT era at 10^{-43} seconds after the Big Bang, right up to the magic moment when zero seconds had elapsed after the birth of the universe, we come to a state that physicists refer to as the *singularity*. The singularity occurred when all of the matter of the universe was—theoretically, at least—in a state of infinite density. Since infinite density is a state that cannot be understood in terms of modern physics, it is regarded as a singular state indeed; hence the term "singularity."

Our inability to understand the singularity is, at least in part, a result of our inability to create a satisfactory description of gravity in quantum terms, rather than in Einstein's relativistic terms. Because we cannot describe it in quantum terms, we cannot yet show what the universe would have been like when gravity was unified with the other three forces—the strong force, the electromagnetic force, and the weak force. This unification would have only lasted for the first 10^{-43} seconds after the Big Bang, but it would have been the state in which our universe was born.

When we do have a proper quantum understanding of gravity (and such an understanding may well arise either from supersymmetry or from the superstring theory), then we might find that the singularity is just an illusion, a product of our incomplete understanding of the conditions that existed at the birth of the universe. Perhaps there never was a state of infinite density. In fact, it may be possible that the universe in the first 10^{-43} seconds of its existence did not contain any matter at all!

No matter at all? If this is so, then where did the matter that we see about us today come from? Well, we've already seen that matter can be created out of the virtual particles in the vacuum if there's enough energy present to make the conversion possible, so perhaps the real question is: Where did the energy come from?

One of the most startling answers to this question comes from an exciting new theory that almost magically answers many of the questions that cosmologists have asked about the origin of our universe. It is called the *inflationary universe hypothesis.* It was proposed in 1979 by a young physicist named Alan Guth. The details of this theory are still being worked out today.

*The American physicist Alan Guth proposed
the inflationary universe hypothesis.*

The basic idea of the inflationary universe hypothesis is that the universe has not always expanded at the same speed. There may have been a period, immediately after the Big Bang, when it expanded at a rate vastly greater than the rate at which it is expanding today. Borrowing a term from economics, cosmologists refer to this period of rapid expansion as *cosmic inflation*. This inflationary era would have been brief, lasting no more than a fraction of a second, but it would have been responsible for the creation of all of the energy, and therefore matter, that exists in the universe today.

How can energy be created? Doesn't that go against everything we have had to say so far about the symmetry of the universe? Read on.

The key to the inflationary universe is the so-called *false vacuum state*. We saw in Chapter Three that a vacuum, far from being empty, is filled with virtual particles. Thus, physicists cannot define the vacuum as being in a state of emptiness. Rather, because the virtual particles that make up the vacuum do not have the energy that they need to become real particles, physicists define the vacuum as a state of minimum energy.

When you pick up a ball and hold it above the ground, you are increasing its state of potential energy; you are putting it into a higher energy state. But the moment you let go of the ball, it will convert that potential energy into kinetic energy and return to a lower energy state; that is, it will fall to the ground. (In fact, physicists refer to the lowest energy state that anything can take as the *ground state*.) We can say that all objects in the universe tend to seek their state of lowest energy, unless something (such as the hand with which you are holding the ball) blocks them from doing so.

The vacuum of space normally exists in the ground state, but it is possible, in theory at least, for it to enter a higher energy state. Ordinarily, it would return immediately to the ground state, seeking its state of lowest energy. But it is theoretically possible that it could become stuck in a higher energy state just as the ball becomes temporarily stuck in your hand when you hold it above the ground. This higher energy state is called the false vacuum.

When Guth worked out the symmetry equations describing the universe in a false vacuum state, he made the amazing discovery that it would have been possible for the universe to produce unlimited amounts of energy while in this state and yet not violate the law of the conservation of energy. This energy would have taken the form of an extremely rapid expansion of space itself. Guth hypothesized that this state of rapid expansion, which he called the inflationary phase, took place almost immediately after the Big Bang. In fact, this inflationary phase may have *been* the Big Bang and may explain why the universe started expanding in the first place.

The false vacuum is inherently unstable. Although something, not yet fully understood, was preventing the universe from reaching the true vacuum state—that is, the state in which the vacuum is truly at minimum energy—this blockage would have quickly degenerated, and the universe would have dropped into the true vacuum state, probably after only a tiny fraction of a second had passed. The expansion of the universe today is only a tiny remnant of the expansion that began during the false vacuum state.

But as inflation ended and the expansion slowed down, the energy created during the inflationary phase did not just go away; instead, it was converted into matter, causing vast numbers of virtual particles in the newly expanded universe to become real particles. Before the inflationary phase, the universe had been empty, in the sense that all of its particles were virtual ones. But after inflation they suddenly became real, and the eras that we described in the previous chapter began.

Interestingly, the inflationary universe hypothesis answers a question that we introduced way back in Chapter Two: Why is the universe so smooth? We suggested then that it seemed odd that the composition of the universe was so even throughout, despite the fact that large portions of the universe would never have been together at any time since the Big Bang, given the speed at which the universe was thought to be expanding. But if the universe was once expanding at a speed greater than that at which it is known to be expanding today, it is possible that the entire visible universe (and much outside of it) would have been together at a time just after the Big Bang. Thus, the universe could have been mixed together smoothly like the water in our hypothetical bathtub (see Chapter Two) and still spread apart rapidly enough by cosmic inflation so that widely spaced areas of the universe would still have the same essential character and general smoothness.

Nonetheless, the inflationary universe theory also raises some questions. For instance, why did the universe enter the false vacuum state in the first place? No one knows, though it may eventually be possible to answer this question. Perhaps an even more interesting question is: What was the universe like before the inflationary phase? If the inflationary phase *was* the Big Bang, then the question becomes: What happened before the Big Bang?

According to the supersymmetry and superstring theories, the universe is eleven-dimensional, with ten dimensions of space and one dimension of time. When we speak of the expansion of the universe, however, it is only three of the space dimensions that are believed to be expanding. The other seven space dimensions remain precisely the same size. (The time dimension, of course, seems to play by different rules.)

Before the Big Bang, all ten of the space dimensions may have been the same size. Then some cosmic disaster came along—perhaps the false vacuum state that initiated the inflationary phase we just discussed—causing three of these ten dimensions to tear away from the others and enter a state of runaway expansion. They are still expanding today.

And yet, according to the most advanced theories of physics being formulated today, we are still aware of these other dimensions. They manifest themselves as the forces of nature, mediating interactions between particles. In a real way, they are still part of our universe; they make our universe the way it is.

How big was the universe before the Big Bang? By most estimates, it would have been 10^{-33} centimeters in diameter, or .000000000000000000000000000000001 centimeters. The seven nonexpanding dimensions would still be this size today. And where was the universe at the time of the Big Bang? In a sense, it was everywhere. Even if our universe today has a finite size, there is no point within it that can be said to be the center of the universe. In fact, the center of the universe is everywhere—and nowhere. Just as the seven miniature dimensions now exist at every point in space, so the center of our universe—the point from which the universe is expanding—is at every point in space.

It is even possible that our universe is a single, eleven-dimensional virtual particle that exists—or once existed—as part of an even larger universe. Somehow this virtual particle, or three dimensions of it, got stuck in the false vacuum state and began to expand. Just as a single virtual particle in our universe can turn into a real particle when it receives enough energy, so this virtual particle from some "superuniverse" might have received enough energy through inflation to turn into *our* universe! And, if this was the case, then ours may not be the only universe that exists. The super-universe may be a seething ocean of expanding universes, the way that our universe is a seething ocean of virtual particles. Instead of being a unique event, our universe may be just one of an uncountable number of universes. Or, as physicist Edward Tryon put it, "our universe is simply one of those things that happens from time to time."[2]

THERE IS an interesting footnote to the inflationary hypothesis that should give everybody pause to reflect about the ultimate fate of our universe. When the universe was in the false vacuum state, it was a very different place than it is today. Not only was it empty of matter and expanding at a very much faster rate, but the laws of the universe were different than they are today. Matter as we know it—and, therefore, stars, galaxies, and life itself—could not have existed in the inflationary universe. It can only exist in the true vacuum state, which the universe is in today.

But a few physicists have questioned whether or not the universe is actually in the true vacuum state today. Perhaps, when the original false vacuum state ended, the universe simply fell into another false vacuum state, and we are still in that false vacuum state today. Although the vacuum is currently in a much lower energy state than it was in during the inflationary period, it is not yet in the ground state. There may be another state of even lower energy than this one. And one day the universe may fall into it, the way a ball may fall off the top of a table after sitting on it for many years, when someone accidentally kicks the table leg. (And, given the strange random fuzziness of the quantum world, it may not even be necessary for someone to kick the "table leg" of the universe. It may just happen, all by itself, quite spontaneously. The universe may, as physicists like to put it, "tunnel through" to the true vacuum state, just as the hydrogen nuclei in the core of the sun tunnel through the electromagnetic force so that fusion can take place.)

If the universe then enters a new vacuum state, a different set of rules may come into existence. It may no longer be possible for the universe to support stars, galaxies—and life. We will suddenly cease to exist, along with everything else in the universe. For what it's worth, the change would take place so suddenly that we would never be aware that it had happened, but that's certainly small consolation. On the more encouraging side, we can note that it hasn't happened for the 18 billion years or so that the universe has existed already, so there's no reason to assume that it will happen in the near future, or that it will happen at all. But no one can prove that it will not happen.

Assuming that we really are in the true vacuum state and that the universe can be expected to go on in its current state for much of the foreseeable future, what will be the ultimate fate of the universe? In a book that talks about the birth of our universe, it seems only fair that we also take a brief look at the possible other end of our existence. Just what does the birth of the universe tell us about the way in which our universe will possibly die? That will be the subject of the last chapter of this book. First, however, let's look at some alternative theories of the universe's origin, theories that do not necessarily begin with a bang.

SEVEN

ALTERNATIVE THEORIES

Most astronomers today would agree that the universe as we know it began with the Big Bang. Nonetheless, there are other theories that attempt to explain the universe that we see about us, and some of these theories don't involve the Big Bang (or even big bangs). Some don't even involve an expanding universe.

In order to be accepted by the scientific community, a theory must offer a satisfactory explanation of observed phenomena. The Big Bang theory is successful because it explains much of what astronomers observe when they peer into space with their telescopes. In particular, it explains the red-shifted light from distant galaxies and the cosmic background radiation detected by Penzias and Wilson. Nonetheless, there are certain facts that the Big Bang theory does not explain.

One of these is the way in which galaxies formed in the early years of the universe's existence. As we saw in Chapter Five, the very early universe was extremely homogenous, that is, it was a smooth soup of particles without any "lumps" in it. We can verify this smoothness by examining the cosmic background radiation, which is exactly the same strength in every direction that we look, at least within the limits of our ability to measure it. Yet the present universe is full of "lumps": stars, galaxies, clusters of galaxies, even clusters of clusters of galaxies. How did we get from there to here?

The Big Bang theory doesn't say. Most cosmologists believe that there were tiny fluctuations in density—lumps—in the early universe that eventually grew into the big fluctuations that we see today. These fluctuations were too small for us to detect evidence of them in the cosmic background radiation. The problem with this notion is that such tiny fluctuations would have taken a very long time to grow into the clusters of galaxies that we see today, and the Big Bang theory doesn't allow that much time.

Eventually, scientists may find a way around this problem, but there are a few maverick theorists who believe that this represents a fundamental flaw in the Big Bang theory. For this and other reasons, they have developed alternative theories of the universe.

The most famous alternative theory of the universe is the so-called steady-state theory, proposed in 1948 by British cosmologists Fred Hoyle, Thomas Gold, and Herman Bondi. When the steady-state theory was devised, it was believed that the Big Bang had occurred only a few billion years ago, perhaps slightly *after* the origin of our own solar system. Since this was obviously ridiculous, the British cosmologists postulated a universe without a beginning, a universe that had existed forever. According to steady-state theory, the universe has always looked exactly as it does today, and it will always look that way. There is no need to explain the origin of galaxies and clusters of galaxies because they have always existed; they had no origin.

How does the steady-state theory explain the red-shifted light from distant galaxies? According to Hoyle (so to speak), the universe is indeed expanding, because of the inherent instability first noted by Einstein in his General Theory of Relativity, but it is not becoming less dense. How can the universe expand without becoming less dense? The steady-state theory says that matter is constantly being created out of empty space, providing material for new stars and galaxies to fill in the spaces between the expanding older ones.

But doesn't this defy the law of the conservation of mass/energy, which says that matter and energy can never be created or destroyed? Yes, but Hoyle was quick to remind other scientists that the law of the conservation of mass/energy is deemed true only because scientists have never observed it being violated. We saw in Chapter Three that matter and energy can come into existence as long as it

*Fred Hoyle, a British astronomer, has
proposed an alternative theory of
the universe—the steady-state theory.*

happens in such a way that physicists cannot observe it happening. The steady-state theory suggests that the amount of new matter necessary to balance out the expansion of the universe would be so small that we cannot observe it with our present instruments.

How much matter would need to be created in order to keep an expanding universe at a constant density? Roughly one proton per year per square kilometer.

As it became apparent that the universe was several billion years older than was at first thought, the steady-state theory rapidly lost adherents. The discovery of the cosmic background radiation, which the steady-state theory cannot explain, was also devastating to the theory. Few scientists support the steady-state theory today.

Nonetheless, some variations on the steady-state theory yet survive. Perhaps the most popular of these at the moment is the theory devised by plasma physicist Hannes Alfven and colleagues, which suggests that the expanding universe is a local explosion taking place in a much larger universe. This explosion, according to Alfven, was caused by large amounts of matter encountering large amounts of antimatter. In Alfven's view, the universe is composed of roughly equal amounts of each type of particle.

We saw earlier, however, that such a matter-antimatter universe is extremely unlikely. Scientists would certainly be able to detect the radiation produced by the zones in space where matter particles and antimatter particles are presently encountering, and annihilating, one another. Yet such radiation has never been detected.

Alfven's theory of matter-antimatter explosions was devised in support of a more strongly grounded theory in which galaxies and clusters of galaxies are viewed as having been formed by electric currents traveling through the thin medium of particles that fills the universe. There is some evidence for such electrically guided galaxy formation, but like other types of galaxy formation, it would have taken more time than is available in a universe that began with the Big Bang. Hence, Alfven has dispensed with the Big Bang and proposed that the universe exists in a more or less steady state.

Some theorists have even suggested that the universe is not expanding at all. How do these theorists explain the red-shifted light from distant galaxies? Some suggest that it is the result of "tired light," that is, light that has lost energy after traveling huge distances across space. There is no evidence that light loses energy with distance, but there is no way at present to prove that it does not. Hence, these theories are interesting but inconclusive.

Other theorists suggest that the universe is expanding and that the Big Bang actually did take place but not in the way that we have described in the last two chapters. One theory says that the early universe, rather than being extremely hot, was extremely cold. This helps to explain the formation of galaxies—cold matter clumps together more readily than hot matter—but not the cosmic background radiation.

Perhaps the most bizarre but fascinating variant on the Big Bang theory is that devised by British physicist-cosmologist Stephen Hawking, who has proposed that the universe exists in a kind of closed time-loop, which keeps returning to the Big Bang again and again. When the universe reaches its point of maximum expansion, Hawking suggests, time begins running backward—until the Big Bang occurs again, and time once more begins running forward. To the inhabitants of such a time-reversed universe, nothing would seem unusual, since they could only perceive time as running forward, no matter in which direction it was actually running. (In fact, there is some question as to whether the notion of "backward time" has any meaning at all.) There is no way to tell, for instance, whether time is currently running forward or backward.

Hawking's theory has the advantage of avoiding the "singularity"—that is, the point of infinite density—with which the traditional Big Bang theory says the universe began. In Hawking's vision, time would reverse itself just before the singularity

The British physicist-cosmologist Stephen Hawking developed a variation on the Big Bang theory.

was reached. Since the singularity is considered bothersome by most physicists, this is a point in Hawking's favor.

Still other theorists have suggested that there was not just one Big Bang but many—a kind of "bang-bang-bang" theory, as one scientist has described it—and that there will be many more Big Bangs in the future. This suggestion, however, leads us into a completely different topic, which we will discuss in the next chapter. How will the universe end? Is this the only universe that will ever exist? Or will there be many more universes, one after another, for the rest of time?

———————— *EIGHT*————————

ENDINGS

The Big Bang theory tells us that the universe has existed for a finite amount of time. In other words, the universe had a beginning. Are we to assume, then, that it will also have an end? Or will it go on existing forever?

No one knows for sure, but the key to this question lies in a subject we discussed way back in Chapter Two: Is the universe open, closed, or flat?

You'll recall that an open universe is infinite in size, a closed universe is finite in size, and a flat universe is balanced precisely between these two alternatives. Similarly, an open universe will have an infinite lifetime, a closed universe will have a finite lifetime, and a flat universe will have a lifetime that is not quite either.

The fate of the universe, then, depends on how much matter there is in the universe—or, more precisely, how densely packed that matter is, as we explained in Chapter Two. If there is enough matter to make it closed, the universe will eventually stop expanding and collapse back in on itself, like a star imploding into a black hole. If there isn't enough matter to close the universe, then it will continue expanding forever, until all the stars have burned out. If there is just enough matter to make it flat, then it will eventually stop expanding, but it will do so only after an infinite amount of time has passed, so that no recollapse will be possible.

Alas, we do not yet know how much matter there is in the universe (or how densely packed it is). Thus, we have to consider all three possible alternatives for the universe's future—though, as we shall see in a moment, some of the recent theories of the universe's origin cast a revealing light on its fate. First, however, let's look at what each of these possibilities might be like.

The Closed Universe. If the universe is closed, then it will eventually stop expanding and recollapse. How long will it take before this recollapse occurs? That depends on how much matter there is in the universe. A few theorists have gone so far as to give specific figures for the end of expansion, some as little as 28 billion years. But this could be much too short a time. Figures in the trillions of years have also been cited.

Once the expansion stops, the collapse will go on for as long as the expansion did. Astronomers in this far-off future universe will first notice that the distant galaxies are no longer red-shifted, then that they have actually become blue-shifted. The matter in the universe will start becoming denser. If the universe has a finite size, it will start to grow smaller.

As the collapsing universe grows denser, the cosmic microwave background radiation will grow hotter. At the present time, the photons in this radiation have an average temperature of approximately 3 degrees Kelvin, that is, 3 degrees above absolute zero. As the universe collapses, however, and these photons find themselves trapped in a smaller and smaller "box," their temperature will increase, just as their temperature decreased as the universe expanded. Not only will the collapsing universe become smaller, it will also become hotter.

This increase in heat will be insignificant to all except radio astronomers for some billions of years. As the universe becomes extremely small— or, at least, extremely dense—this heat will become noticeable even to those not attuned to the activities of photons in space. As seen from the surface of the earth (or any other planet for that matter), the sky will actually start to glow.

By this time, however, a number of other significant changes will have taken place in the universe. The space between the galaxies would have been squeezed out of existence, and the galaxies themselves would begin to merge into one giant supergalaxy. The universe would be a vast sea of stars without any larger structures, much the way astronomers before the mid-1920s envisioned the universe of today.

As space itself grows hotter, even stars will cease to exist. In order to continue its existence, a star must lose the heat that it produces into the cold vacuum of space. In today's universe, this is a simple matter, since space is barely warmer than absolute zero. But as the temperature of the cosmic background radiation increases, space itself will eventually become hotter than the surface of a star. Unable to lose their heat to space, stars will first expand like balloons filled with hot air and then begin to boil away into nothing. Alternatively, the pressure of the particles that make up the background radiation of space may prevent the stars from boiling away and cause them to collapse instead, so that the universe will become filled with black holes.

By this time, however, it is unlikely that there will be any human astronomers around to survey the state of the universe. If any humans have survived the gradual heating of the universe, they will have been driven underground or into elaborately contrived shelters in order to withstand the worsening conditions in the universe. But even the strongest of shelters can protect the surviving humans from the increasing heat and radiation of the universe for only so long. Before the collapse is complete, humans (and all other forms of life in the universe) will be incinerated.

The universe will then enter a phase that cosmologists like to call the *Big Crunch*—the Big Bang in reverse gear. The universe will, as far as we know, collapse into a state of infinite density, a singularity. Of course, as we saw in the last chapter, singularities may not really exist. Until a quantum theory of gravity is developed, however, cosmologists will be unable to say what actually will take place at the very end of the universe's existence.

One possibility, which has long fascinated cosmologists, is that the universe may explode once again in another Big Bang. A brand-new universe might be created, which may be very much like the universe in which we live, or completely different. That universe would then collapse in another Big Crunch, which would then lead to another Big Bang, and so forth. Potentially, this process could go on forever and may have been going on forever in the past. We may not be the first universe that has existed and we may not be the last.

As appealing as this scenario might sound, there is a flaw in it. The science of thermodynamics, which describes the way in which energy changes form over time, tells us that the energy that goes into making the universe expand would be reduced a little with each new Big Bang. Eventually, the universe would get "tired" and would no longer keep exploding. Thus, the idea of an infinite number of Big Bangs, stretching backward and forward in time, is not likely to be the case. More likely, our Big Bang is the only Big Bang that has happened so far and may well be the last.

Open or Flat Universe. If the universe is open—or even if it is flat—there will be no Big Crunch. The universe will never recollapse. It will exist forever. Interestingly, the equations of the inflationary universe hypothesis state that the universe *must* be flat; this is the only possible result of cosmic inflation, which explains why the observed matter density of the universe is so close to that required to *make* it flat, as we commented in Chapter Two. If inflation is correct, then, there never will be a Big Crunch.

But neither will the universe remain forever in its current state. Eventually, even the stars must burn out. And, if the current grand unification theories are correct, even matter itself will fall apart sooner or later.

What will the future of an open universe be like? As far as we know, the universe will remain pretty much as it is now for a very long time. Our sun will burn out in about 5 billion years, but other stars much like it will be born from clouds of gas and dust to take its place. If the human race is still around, it will probably have abandoned our solar system for the planets of these younger stars long before our sun meets its ultimate fate.

But there is only so much energy available in the universe for the building of new stars. Just as the laws of thermodynamics tell us that a closed universe can't go on collapsing and expanding forever, so they tell us that new stars cannot go on being created forever in an open universe. Eventu-

*From this fifteenth-century discussion
between Theologian and Astronomer
to the current debates and speculation,
we have come far in our understanding
of the universe.*

ally, the last star will die out and will not be replaced.

Different stars have different lifetimes. Larger stars burn hotter and therefore burn out sooner than smaller stars. Within approximately 100 trillion years, however, not only will all the stars in existence today have used up their fuel, but there will not be enough hydrogen—the raw material of stars—left in the universe to create new ones. The universe will be filled with white dwarfs, neutron stars, and black holes. A few of these may still glow dimly, but even that last flicker of light will eventually disappear.

This will not be the true end of the universe, however. In Chapter Four, we saw that even the most stable of all hadrons—the proton—will eventually decay. After about a billion billion billion billion years, all atoms will fall apart, and matter as we know it will cease to exist. The universe will be a vast sea of leptons and messenger particles.

This sounds like a pretty dull universe, but there may still be some excitement in store. It is possible for two kinds of leptons, electrons and antielectrons (or positrons), to form a new kind of "atom," known as a *positronium* atom. There is a theory that suggests that huge atoms of positronium will form in the universe after a billion billion billion billion billion years or so have passed. Each one of these positronium atoms will be larger than the entire visible universe is today, but by this time the universe will be so large (even if it has a finite size) that it will be able to accommodate huge numbers of these atoms.

Is it possible for matter to form from positronium atoms? No one knows, but it's interesting to speculate about what such a positronium future might be like. If positronium matter can form, then it is remotely possible that something analogous to stars, planets, and even living creatures may evolve in that distant future, on a scale of size vastly larger than the observable universe today. Living positronium beings would be so large that light would take billions and billions of years to travel the distance from their hands to their eyes— if such beings have hands and eyes.

You might ask how any being could survive if the messages carried in light took that long to reach them from an object they might be looking at. But bear in mind that the signals that carry thoughts through such a being's brain would be equally slowed down by its huge size. Thus, billions of years in this distant future universe would seem like tiny fractions of a second to a positronium being, and this slowness of perception would be precisely balanced by the slowness of everything else in the positronium universe. To a positronium being, the universe might look pretty much like the universe looks to us, despite its vastly larger (and slower) scale.

Fortunately, an open universe would give even such incredibly slow beings plenty of time to evolve and prosper, to build empires and create art, to explore space, and to theorize about the origin of the universe. In fact, to these positronium beings it would seem as though *we* had existed in the first fraction of a second after the Big Bang. Probably, they would not guess that we had existed at all. After all, how could living beings evolve and thrive in such a tiny amount of time?

And now that we have speculated about positronium beings whose lifetimes span unbelievably large numbers of years, let's turn our speculation back to the beginning of our own universe. Is it possible that in the first fraction of a second after the birth of our universe—when matter was incredibly dense, different forces of nature existed, and different kinds of particles emerged from the vacuum particles of the void—that there could also have been something in that incredible density of matter analogous to the stars and planets of today? Could living creatures, perhaps constructed from free quarks, have evolved and thrived in that tiny fraction of a second, just as we have evolved in the first fraction of a second of the positronium beings' universe?

Looked at in that light, it becomes more obvious why cosmologists think of the origin of our universe in terms of "eras," even when those eras are a tiny fraction of a second long. There may not have been living beings in the incredibly dense universe of those first few seconds—though it would be difficult at present to prove that there weren't—but in some ways more happened in the universe during those seconds than has happened in all the time since.

By understanding those few seconds in which the universe came to be, we come to a better understanding of the universe itself. And by understanding the universe, perhaps we will eventually come to an understanding of the position that we occupy within it, somewhere between the quarks and the positronium. In the origin of matter and forces in the Big Bang, we inevitably find the origin of everything that we see about us today, including the most miraculous thing of all: thinking beings who are actually capable of understanding the universe in which they live.

GLOSSARY

antimatter—matter constructed out of particles that are identical to those that constitute ordinary matter in all ways except electric charge.

asymmetry—the absence of symmetry.

Big Bang—colloquial name for the explosion that is believed to have marked the origin of the universe and initiated its present expansion.

Big Crunch—the hypothetical scenario in which the universe is depicted as eventually collapsing in a reverse Big Bang.

black dwarf—a white dwarf that has cooled off to the point that it no longer produces light.

black hole—the (theoretical) remains of a star that has succumbed to a tremendous supernova explosion, causing the core to collapse to such extreme density that its gravitational attraction prevents even light from escaping its surface.

blue shift—a Doppler shift in the wavelength of light toward the blue end of the spectrum, indicating that the source of the light is moving closer to the observer (or vice versa).

cepheid variables—stars that change their brightness over predictable intervals of time.

closed universe—the theoretical model of the universe that depicts the overall curvature of space as being closed into a sphere and suggests that the universe will eventually recollapse under its own gravitational attraction.

cosmic egg—name sometimes applied to the highly compressed universe that presumably existed at the time of the Big Bang.

cosmic microwave background radiation—microwave radiation permeating all of space, left over from the period shortly after the Big Bang.

cosmic strings—large, theoretical "cracks" in the fabric of the universe, formed shortly after the Big Bang and manifesting themselves as extremely dense strings generating immense amounts of gravity.

cosmological constant—a term introduced by Albert Einstein in his General Theory of Relativity in order to prevent the theoretical universe depicted in his equations from expanding or collapsing; later regarded by Einstein as the greatest mistake of his career.

cosmology—the field of science that studies the origin, evolution, and large-scale structure of the universe.

Doppler effect—the phenomenon by which waves of sound or light change their apparent wavelengths when measured by an observer moving relative to the source of the waves.

electric charge—a property of certain subatomic particles that determines how they interact electromagnetically.

electromagnetic force—one of the four forces by which particles interact with each other; electromagnetic interactions are governed by the property, possessed by certain subatomic particles, of electric charge.

electromagnetic radiation—the various types of radiation, including visible light, infrared, ultraviolet and microwave radiation, television and radio waves, gamma rays, and X rays.

electron—one of the three subatomic particles that constitute the entities we call atoms.

electroweak era—the period shortly after the Big Bang during which the electromagnetic and weak forces were indistinguishable from one another, but when both were distinguished from the strong force.

electroweak force—the single force that manifests itself as both the electromagnetic and weak forces.

fission—the process by which the nuclei of large, unstable atoms, such as atoms of plutonium or of certain isotopes of uranium, break apart to form the nuclei of smaller, more stable atoms, releasing energy as they do so.

flat universe—the theoretical model of the universe in which the universe has no overall curvature and in which it will stop expanding only after an infinite amount of time has elapsed.

forces—term used to describe the four basic ways in which subatomic particles can interact with one another, specifically electromagnetism, gravity, the strong force, and the weak force; now believed to be four manifestations of a single, underlying superforce.

fusion—the process by which smaller atoms join together to form larger atoms, releasing energy as they do so; see also *hydrogen fusion*.

galactic cluster—a large body of galaxies bound together gravitationally.

galactic halo—a donut-shaped body of invisible matter that some astronomers believe may surround the visible bodies of most galaxies.

galaxy—a large body of stars bound together gravitationally, often in the shape of a large spiral or ellipse.

grand unification era—the period immediately after the Big Bang during which the electromagnetic, weak, and strong forces were indistinguishable from one another; also called the GUT era.

grand unification temperature—the temperature at which the electromagnetic, weak, and strong forces become indistinguishable from one another; approximately 1,000,000,000,000,000 (one million billion) degrees Kelvin.

grand unification theory (GUT)—any theory that attempts to unite the electromagnetic, weak, and strong forces as manifestations of a single underlying force.

gravity—one of the four forces through which subatomic particles interact; although it is the weakest of the four, the ability of gravity to work over extremely long distances makes it an important force, holding planets, stars, solar systems, galaxies, and clusters of galaxies together.

ground state—the state of minimum energy.

GUT *freezing*—the moment shortly after the Big Bang when the strong force became distinguishable ("froze out") from the electromagnetic and weak forces.

hadron era—the period shortly after the Big Bang during which quarks were first bound into hadrons.

hadrons—particles of matter, such as neutrons and protons, that are made from smaller particles called quarks; see also *leptons*.

Heisenberg uncertainty principle—the principle, discovered by

German physicist Wernher Heisenberg, that states (roughly speaking) that we cannot have perfect knowledge of any particle; for instance, we cannot simultaneously know both the position and momentum of a particle to an arbitrary degree of certainty.

hydrogen fusion—the process by which stars (and hydrogen bombs) produce energy (heat and light) by fusing hydrogen atoms into helium atoms.

inflationary universe hypothesis—theory that depicts the early universe as having expanded at a much greater rate than it is expanding today.

interstellar medium—a thin cloud of gas and dust that pervades interstellar space.

invisible matter—see *missing mass*.

kinetic energy—energy of motion.

lepton era—the period shortly after the Big Bang during which the overall energy density of the universe was sufficient to create leptons out of the vacuum but insufficient to create hadrons.

leptons—particles of matter, such as the electron and the neutrino, that are not made of quarks; see also *hadrons*.

light-year—the distance that light travels in a year, roughly equivalent to 6 trillion miles; commonly used as a measure of cosmological distances.

matter era—the period beginning several hundred thousand years after the Big Bang during which the majority of the energy in the universe became bound up in matter; we are still in the matter era today.

mirror symmetry—the property of an entity that allows it to remain unchanged even if its left and right halves are reversed, as in a mirror.

missing mass—the mass that some cosmologists and astronomers believe the universe must have in order to explain certain observations of galaxies and other gravitationally bound bodies; presumably, this mass is invisible at standard radiation frequencies, because it has not yet been observed through conventional observational techniques; also called invisible matter.

nebula (pl., nebulae)—a cloud of gas and dust in outer space.

neutron—one of the three subatomic particles that constitute the entities we call atoms.

nucleons—collective term for neutrons and protons, because they are the particles that constitute the nucleus of the atom.

nucleus—the central core of an atom.

Olbers's paradox—the observation, credited to the nineteenth-century astronomer Heinrich Olbers but actually much older, that if the universe were infinitely large, infinitely old, and evenly filled with stars, then the night sky could not possibly be dark because there would be stars in every direction that we looked, rather than a relatively few stars scattered about the sky.

open universe—the theoretical model of the universe that depicts the overall curvature of space as being open like an infinitely extended saddle, and suggests that the universe will continue expanding forever.

particle accelerators—machines used by physicists to examine subatomic particles by colliding them with one another at high speeds and studying the results.

photon—the particle of light and other forms of electromagnetic radiation; also, the "messenger particle" that carries the electromagnetic force.

photon era—the period after the Big Bang, following the wholesale matter-antimatter annihilation of hadrons and leptons, during which the universe was dominated by photons. In some ways, we are still in the photon era today, although the energy content of these ancient photons is now extremely low, and so the current era is generally accepted to be the matter era, with most energy bound up in matter.

potential energy—energy of position.

proton—one of the three subatomic particles that constitute the entities we call atoms.

quantum mechanics—the study of the elementary particles and forces that constitute our universe at its simplest level.

quarks—the small particles from which certain larger particles—in particular, the neutrons and protons—are formed.

red shift—a Doppler shift in the wavelength of light toward the red end of the spectrum, indicating that the source of the light is moving away from the observer (or vice versa).

reductionism—the philosophy that everything in the universe can be explained by one or a few underlying principles.

rotational symmetry—the property of an entity that allows it to remain unchanged after being rotated.

singularity—a point in space or time at which the density of matter is so great that the known laws of physics break down; possibly the result of physicists' inability to find a quantum description of gravity and thus unify gravity with the other three forces of nature.

steady-state theory—an alternative to the Big Bang theory that suggests that the universe has always been (and will always be) in its current state, with new matter periodically being created out of the vacuum to maintain the matter density as the universe expands.

strong force—one of the four forces by which particles interact with each other; among other things, the strong force binds the neutrons and protons in place within the atomic nucleus.

subatomic particles—particles that are smaller than (and, in some cases, part of) the atoms that make up the material elements.

superclusters—clusters of galactic clusters bound together gravitationally.

superstring theory—one of several theories that attempt to unite the electromagnetic, weak, strong, and gravitational forces as manifestations of a single underlying superforce; string theory postulates that the most fundamental subatomic particles are actually minuscule "strings."

supersymmetry—one of several theories that attempt to unite the electromagnetic, weak, strong, and gravitational forces as manifestations of a single underlying force.

symmetry—the property of an entity that allows it to remain apparently unchanged by rotations or alterations of its position or state.

unified field theory—a theory that depicts one or more of the forces of nature as manifestations of a single underlying force.

vacuum fluctuations—the constant appearance and disappearance of virtual particles out of a seemingly empty vacuum.

virtual particles—particles that appear out of the seemingly empty vacuum of space and disappear again before they can be detected experimentally.

weak force—one of the four forces by which particles interact with each other; the weak force is responsible for certain interactions in which particles change into other types of particles.

white dwarf—the extremely dense remains of a star that has ended its fusion-burning lifetime and collapsed to a fraction of its former size.

NOTES AND
SOURCES USED

1. Steven Weinberg, *The First Three Minutes* (New York: Bantam, 1979), p. 98.
2. Quoted in James Trefil, *The Moment of Creation* (New York: Charles Scribner's Sons, 1983), p. 208.

Barrow, John D., and Joseph Silk. *The Left Hand of Creation: The Origin and Evolution of the Expanding Universe.* New York: Basic Books, 1983.
Bernstein, Jeremy. *Three Degrees Above Absolute Zero: Bell Labs in the Information Age.* New York: Charles Scribner's Sons, 1984.
Chaisson, Eric. *Cosmic Dawn: The Origins of Matter and Life.* New York: Little, Brown & Co., 1981.
Davies, Paul. *Superforce: The Search for a Grand Unified Theory of Nature.* New York: Simon & Schuster, 1984.
Gribbon, John. *In Search of the Big Bang: Quantum Physics and Cosmology.* New York: Bantam, 1986.
Harrison, Edward R. *Cosmology: The Science of the Universe.* Cambridge: Cambridge University Press, 1981.
Hawking, Stephen. *A Brief History of Time: From the Big Bang to Black Holes.* New York: Bantam, 1988.
Kaku, Dr. Michio, and Jennifer Trainer. *Beyond Einstein: The Cosmic Quest for the Theory of the Universe.* New York: Bantam, 1987.

Morris, Richard. *The Fate of the Universe*. New York: Playboy Press, 1982.

Pagels, Heinz R. *Perfect Symmetry: The Search for the Beginning of Time*. New York: Simon & Schuster, 1985.

Preiss, Byron, ed. *The Universe*. New York: Bantam, 1987.

Rothman, Tony. "This Is the Way the World Ends." *Discover* (July 1987), pp. 82–93.

Silk, Joseph. *The Big Bang: The Creation and Evolution of the Universe*. San Francisco: W. H. Freeman & Co., 1980.

Taubes, Gary. "Everything's Now Tied to Strings." *Discover* (November 1986), pp. 34–56.

Trefil, James S. *The Moment of Creation: Big Bang Physics From Before the First Millisecond to the Present Universe*. New York: Charles Scribner's Sons, 1983.

Weinberg, Steven. *The First Three Minutes: A Modern View of the Origin of the Universe*. New York: Bantam, 1979.

Zee, A. *Fearful Symmetry: The Search for Beauty in Modern Physics*. New York: Macmillan, 1986.

RECOMMENDED READING

There are quite a few popular books available on the subject of cosmology and the Big Bang. But just because they are "popular"—that is, written for an audience of nonscientists—does not make them easy reading. In fact, most of the books listed below can be rather daunting to the casual reader, who might be tempted to pick them up with an eye toward skimming for the good parts. Resist this temptation (except in the Preiss book, which is intended for precisely this kind of reading). If you're really interested in learning more about the birth of our universe and the stunning advances in fundamental physics that have given us insight into such a remote event, be prepared to do a great deal of thinking while you read. And, above all, don't skim. You'll quickly find yourself lost in most of these books if you go more than a paragraph without concentrating on what the author has said. However, the subject is sufficiently fascinating, not to mention important, that the reader willing to give these books the effort that they require and deserve will be amply repaid with an understanding of the universe that philosophers and scientists of centuries (and even decades) past would have loved to possess. Books that are the heaviest going will be noted, but even the easiest are guaranteed to present you with an exciting challenge. None of these books, however, is heavy on technical detail, and no mathematical background is needed to make sense of any of them.

Bernstein, Jeremy. *Three Degrees Above Absolute Zero: Bell Labs in the Information Age* (Charles Scribner's Sons, 1984).

An excellent history of AT&T's Bell Laboratories, relevant here for its detailed biographies of Arno Penzias and Robert Wilson and their discovery of the cosmic background radiation that initiated the modern period of cosmology. In fact, the title of the book refers to the current temperature of this residual radiation from the Big Bang. Light reading compared to some of the books that follow, but written by a physicist who is knowledgeable on the subjects he covers.

Gribbin, John. *In Search of the Big Bang: Quantum Physics and Cosmology* (Bantam, 1986).

An excellent attempt to show how physics and cosmology have evolved together throughout the twentieth century. Gribbin, a physicist-turned-author, does not skimp on the scientific detail, and at times the going may get rough for the reader who isn't interested in the technicalities. But it *is* possible to skim past the thorny parts and enjoy the wonderful historical vignettes that Gribbin has laced throughout the manuscript. The bibliography, complete with Gribbin's detailed comments on his sources, is well worth reading for its own sake and will put you on the trail of several good books not mentioned here.

Hawking, Stephen. *A Brief History of Time: From the Big Bang to Black Holes* (Bantam, 1988).

Possibly the most authoritative popular account available of current unified field theories and their relevance to the origin of the universe. Hawking, a physicist and cosmologist who some observers have likened to Einstein, writes crisply and well for a general audience but does not skimp on the nontechnical scientific detail. Occasionally difficult, but worth reading.

Kaku, Dr. Michio, and Jennifer Trainer. *Beyond Einstein: The Cosmic Quest for the Theory of the Universe* (Bantam, 1987).

As of this writing, the only popular book available on superstring theory. Easier reading than most of the other books in this listing and clearly aimed at an audience without a scientific background, but also rather superficial, especially in the treatment of superstring theory itself (though the authors do an excellent job of placing superstring theory in the general context of modern physics). A good starting point for a reader interested in both cutting-edge physics and the origin of the universe, but should be followed by further reading.

Pagels, Heinz R. *Perfect Symmetry: The Search for the Beginning of Time* (Simon & Schuster, 1985).

Beautifully written and full of fascinating detail about the universe and current scientific thought, this book by a professional physicist is nonetheless rather heavy-going, especially in the latter half, where Pagels tackles some of the most difficult topics in contemporary physics. A good book to read if you're interested in symmetry (or just in astronomy, the subject of the first third of the book), but read the book by Zee (listed in this bibliography) first.

Preiss, Byron, ed. *The Universe* (Bantam, 1987).

The most entertaining of the current books on cosmology and the most appropriate for superficial reading. Editor Preiss has gathered an impressive group of science fact and science fiction writers and put together a fascinating mix of essays and short stories on cosmological topics as varied as "Supernovae and Pulsars," "Intergalactic Matter," and "Other Planets, Other Life." Alan Sandage's essay on "Cosmology" and James Trefil's on "The New Physics and the Universe" provide a good overview of current thought about the Big Bang and the expanding universe. Science fiction writers represented here include Robert Silverberg, David Brin, Gene Wolfe, and Frederik Pohl, with additional factual essays by Ray Bradbury, Isaac Asimov, and many others.

Trefil, James. *The Moment of Creation: Big Bang Physics From Before the First Millisecond to the Present Universe* (Charles Scribner's Sons, 1983).

A detailed description of the Big Bang from a physics teacher who is also a popular science writer. Despite the incredible pace of recent advances in the field, Trefil's book is just recent enough to cover all important developments in this area, with the conspicuous exception of superstring theory. (However, since only one of the volumes in this bibliography devotes more than a page to the brand-new superstring theory, this can hardly be considered a major deficiency in Trefil's book.) Along with the Kaku and Trainer book, this is a good starting point for interested readers.

Weinberg, Steven. *The First Three Minutes* (Bantam Books, 1979).

If there is a single classic of modern Big Bang literature, this is surely it. Written by one of the physicists responsible for the theory of electroweak unification, the picture that Weinberg presents is no longer strictly up-to-date—it lacks some of the most exciting recent ideas, such as superstrings and cosmic inflation—but it is rich with detail. Weinberg explains precisely how cosmologists analyzed the cosmic background radiation discovered by Penzias and Wilson and used this analysis to create a surprisingly detailed and precise description of the hot cosmic "soup" that came into existence a fraction of a second after the Big Bang. A difficult book but worth the effort.

Zee, A. *Fearful Symmetry: The Search for Beauty in Modern Physics* (Macmillan, 1986).

The best book yet published on symmetry as a guiding principle in modern physics. Zee, like Heinz Pagels (above), is an accomplished physicist and his writing here is entertaining and lucid, though much of the subject matter that he has chosen to tackle is difficult. If you have time to read a single book on the subject of symmetry, this is the one to read.

INDEX